TATTERSALL
The Legend

by
Ed Watson
and
Dennis Newlyn

D0027073

Witness Productions
P.O. Box 34, Marshall, IN 47859

© 1991 Witness Productions

Witness Productions
Box 34, Church Street.
Marshall, Indiana 47859

ISBN 0-9627653-1-7

1st printing 1991

Also published in Australia by:
Newlyn Publishing Group
Greenacre, NSW, Australia 2190

Front Cover: The only painting of Bob Tattersall done by Ron Burton
was commissioned by Duke Cook and presented to Delores Tattersall
in memory of her husband. © Ron Burton Ltd., P.O. Box 24342,
Speedway, Indiana 46224

Camera work by Indiana Printing, Crawfordsville, Indiana

Graphic design by The Oman Group, Inc.

Dedicated To
Dee Tattersall
Who loved, lived and shared it with us

In Memory Of

Howard Powers
1926 - 1991
"Chief Goggle Washer"

He left us doing what he loved,
Performing stunts at a Sydney air show

Acknowledgements

This book is a credit to the many writers and photographers who covered Bob Tattersall's career. We have tried to credit every source used in researching the work.

We especially wish to thank Peter Nunn, Dick Jordan and Phil McGee for special contributions.

Thank you to The Oman Group who bailed us out of a difficult situation.

Extreme gratitude to Richard Howell and Indiana Printing.

Love to Ernie and Iris Hopkins and Jane Walters.

To all who sent letters, made phone calls, allowed interviews and helped in researching the story and the race history, we thank you.

American Writers & Sources
Gene Powlen, National Speed Sport News
Wayne Adams, Illustrated Speedway News
Chris Economaki, National Speed Sport News
Dusty Frazer, Stock Car Magazine
Keith Waltz, Speed Sport News
Dick Mittman, Indianapolis News
The Indianapolis News 500 Mile Record Book
Indianapolis Motor Speedway News Dept.
Walter T. Chernokal, Keystone State Comments
Hal Higdon, author "Summer of Triumph"
Jerry Miller, Pit Pass, Chronicle-Tribune
Eileen Terry, Ed Watson's USAC Midget Yearbook
John Mahoney, Racing Pictorial
The Joliet Herald News
The Joliet Public Library

The United States Auto Club
Dick King, President
Dick Jordan, Communications Director
Donald Davidson, Historian
Bill Marvel, V.P./Dir. Corporate Affairs

Australian Writers & Sources
Kym Bonython, Rowley Park Promoter
Kym Bonython, "Ladies' Legs and Lemonade"
Carolyn Sherwood, Bonython Gallery
Dennis Newlyn, Speedway Classics
Bill Lawler, Speedway Classics
Dave Booth, Australian Speedway News
Allan Edworthy, Australian Writer
Australian Speedway Magazine
Sel Harley, President Racing Drivers Assn.

Race History Research
George Sala, Speed Sport News
Bob Mount, AAA-USAC Historian
Bill Hill, Historian
Frank Midgley, Newlyn Publishing Group
Ken Brown, Newlyn Publishing Group
Ernie Wansbone, New Zealand Historian

TATTERSALL The Legend

Others

Paul Baines, USAC Car Owner
Frank Barsi, Bucko
Ted Bohlander, Owner-Driver
Larry Brooks, Fan
Erwin Burris, Owner
Ron Burton, Artist
Mac Campbell, Australian
    Collector
Don Carter, UARA President
The Casey Family
Rhonda Crawford, Friend
Gene Dulin, CORA
    Championship Car Owner
Joe Finley, Car Owner
Jack Feken, Friend
Father John Gaughran
Bobby Grim, Indianapolis Driver
Barry Handlin, NZ-USAC Driver
Bob Higman, Mechanic-Builder
Judy Pierce Hampton
Dale Hampton, Car Owner
"Hacksaw" (Kenny Simmons), a
    Friend
Randy Lewis, Fan

Clifford Ligori
Jeanette Ligori
Mickey Ligori
Mike McGreevy, USAC
    Champion
Leo Melcher, Owner, Promoter,
    Official
Sid Middlemass, Australian
    Driver
Larry Rice, Indianapolis Driver
Charlie Ross, UARA Car Owner
Johnny Shipman, USAC Midget
    Chief Starter
Geoff Spence, Australian Driver
Dave Strickland, USAC Driver
Les Scott, USAC Driver
Tony Saylor, Car Owner
Gerald Á. Santibanes, Fan
Leora Tattersall Angelico
Eleanor Tattersall Caputo
Frank Welch, Mazon Promoter
Aaron Willis, Owner-Driver,
    Official
Leroy Warriner, USAC Midget
    Champion
Bob Wente, Jr., Promoter

Photographers

The photos in this book were acquired from the Dee Tattersall Collection, The Peter Nunn Collection, Rocky Rhodes, The Paul Baines Collection, The Mac Campbell Collection and Kym Bonython's book "Ladies' Legs and Lemonade."

We have tried to credit every photographer whose work appears.

Gail Alloway
Doug Balmer*
David Brock*
Wayne Bryant
Jack Charters
Walter T. Chernokal
David Cumming*
Earl's Racing Photos
K.A. Goodrich
Al J. Herman
Ed Hitze
Bruce Kent*

R.N. Maser, Jr.
Gordon McIsaac[+]
Mike Raymond*
Rocky Rhodes
Ross Photo
Roth Studio
Bob Sheldon
Ian Smith*
Larry Taylor*
Dwight Vaccaro
Howard Weigand
Ed Watson

*Australian photographer
[+]New Zealand

TATTERSALL
The Legend

Introduction

Bob Tattersall......

In the world of midget auto racing that name sends a tingle through the body of thousands of adoring fans around the world.

Bob Tattersall was a man whose deeds on the race track became legendary on both sides of the Pacific. A man with colour, character and personality. Full of charisma long before that descriptive word became fashionable, he was a superstar way ahead of his time.

There are many astute judges in the U.S. who rate Bob Tattersall one of the all time great midget drivers. Standing just under six feet in height, this man of medium build and crew-cut hair was a colossus amongst racing men.

In Australia he was the undisputed king...hailed as the greatest American midget driver ever to race in that country. For thirteen consecutive years he performed in front of packed grandstands at stadiums across the country and thrilled Australian race fans with his own special brand of magic.

Setting records that will never be broken, Tat drove into the hearts of the Aussies...and into history. But whether in Australia, New Zealand or on bull rings of America, the Tattersall racing trademark was always the same. Here was a man who had a fixation about winning. A tough, hard as nails campaigner, a product from the "old school" of hard knocks, and a midget race driver who could not quite accept second best on or off the track.

Like all sportsmen with that special touch, Tattersall was known for his outbursts. Sure he'd cuss and swear and if the situation demanded he could be downright unpleasant. It all went along with the job of buckling into a midget speedcar and running the ragged edge.

Away from the track Bob Tattersall liked his bottle of scotch and loved to party. Here indeed was a man who lived life in the fast lane on and off the track.

Bob Tattersall understood the world of publicity and was a promoter's dream who provided the formula that proved a smashing success at the box office.

His yearly visit to Sydney became a ritual. His introduction to the race fans and following hot laps were a show within a show.

"Good evening ladies and gentlemen. It's great to see so many of you here tonight and it's great to be back in Sydney. I hope I can put on a show for you." The words were simple and to the point. He'd then hand the microphone to the track announcer and walk to the track where the gleaming Offy midget awaited.

Under the glare of track lights and in front of the Sydney press he'd donn the helmet, goggles and face mask, buckle in and prepare to put on a show that left everyone gasping.

The darkness of the huge infield was offset by the ribbon of track lighting. The grandstand lights were switched off and all eyes were on this one car, the chrome glittering under the lights around the circuit.

After some slow laps on the pole line, business time had arrived. Moving to the high line, the crisp bark of the Offenhauser increased.

IT WAS SHOWTIME!

With head tilted back and the tail of the car only inches off the fence, Tat had the Offy in a beautifully controlled slide. Arm movements precise and with a minimum of work of the steering wheel, Bob Tattersall was poetry in motion.

The race line never changed...it was full speed lap after lap, right on the wall. Just beautiful!

As the caution lights came on, the grandstand lighting flickered into life and the applause from the packed stadium erupted over the quieting pitch of the engine.

The workout had come to an end in what also served as the best "psych job" on the opposition one could ever witness. Bob Tattersall, the showman, had scored the first victory of the night.

When Bob first started coming to Australia, advance publicity carried the nick-name "Two Gun." That tag stuck with him throughout his Australian campaign and being portrayed as an American cowboy was played to the fullest.

I am thrilled at the opportunity to join Ed Watson in telling the complete story of the man who became a Legend in my country.

I hope we have done our job and that through our writing "Bob Tattersall, the Legend" will live again.

Dennis Newlyn, publisher
National Speedway Illustrated.

Preface

Who was Bob Tattersall? What made him tick and why did I like him so much?

Understanding the man is what this book is about. When I began to study for the Ministry, I was introduced to a man named King David. As I read about his life and tried to picture him, Bob Tattersall always came to mind. Like King David, Bob Tattersall wasn't afraid of anything.

As I began to compare these two heroes I was awed by how much in common they shared.

The Bob Tattersall I knew was the product of my watching him race as a junior in high school, followed by years as a racing official and writer who helped produce the legend.

For each reader, this book will have a different impact. For his close friends, the toned down language will not project the Tat you knew, and the scripture verses will seem out of place. For the hundreds of kids who chose him as their hero, the exposure of the steamier side of Tat's life may tarnish the image they have carried through the years. For the race fan who watched him race this book will hopefully be interesting.

This story is filled with hundreds of people I have considered great men and women. It also contains the name of the man I consider the greatest man to ever live,

Jesus Christ.

In his last year on this earth, Bob Tattersall also came to this conclusion.

Some will say this book is out of place because Bob Tattersall was not a religious man and feel that I have mixed religion with his life, however, if I am to tell the entire story, this side of Bob's life must be included. The Jesus I know does not like religion any more than Bob did.

Bob and I met Jesus because of a book and it is my hope you will meet the real Bob Tattersall in this book.

There are many who said I could not tell the true story of who Bob Tattersall was, but I feel you will find Tat portrayed on these pages, warts and all.

I knew Bob Tattersall better than most people, but not as well as his closest friends. For each of us who knew him there is an image we have and a legend we believe. Of all who knew the legend, it is Delores Tattersall who lived it with Bob.

Dee has shown great courage in allowing us to see inside their life together.

In all my years I may never be a great writer, but I am pleased with this book because Dee is pleased with it.

Within these pages is the story of a man as shared with us by the people who were closest to him. Bob Tattersall, the man, is revealed through the interviews, notes, clippings, memories, and photos Dee has treasured and retained. It is also the product of, and a tribute to, the many people who report the races, write the columns, shoot the photos and keep the records; people behind the scenes who seldom get credit or pay for their contributions to the sport they love.

Dennis Newlyn and I have tried to credit every person who has aided in any way in telling Bob Tattersall's story. A very special thank you goes to Peter Nunn.

For the fans who love statistics we have tried to include as many races as was humanly possible and wish to thank all who contributed to this search. Most of all I wish to thank Dick Jordan of the United States Auto Club who compiled the entire USAC Record included in this book.

Ed Watson

I have seen a man of valor, a man of war, prudent in speech, and a man of good presence; and the Lord is with him. I Samuel 16:18

1

The Meeting

Turning into the room, Father John's eyes took in the frail form lying on the bed. The sound of heavy labored breathing echoed in a rasping rhythm that was magnified in the small darkened room.

Approaching the bed, the Priest studied the familiar face. The square jaw still prevailed. The deep lines of the face were much deeper and the cheeks sunken. Those dark eyebrows hung down shading the closed eyelids.

"Tat." The words were spoken softly. "It's Father John."

Slowly the eyelids raised like a giant entrance to a deep tunnel.

"Yes, it's still there. That twinkle. That brightness."

That was the most outstanding thing Father John had noticed about this man when he first came to minister to him.

It's the eyes.

The look of eagles.

All great men have it!

The cancer had eaten away and the great Champion was near death's door.

Too weak to talk, a gentle squeeze of the hand told the priest that Tat knew he was here.

Death was close, but death was not the victor. The

eyes told the story. That look of victory was still there. The fans never saw him frail. Even his racing comrades who had come by the hundreds to the benefit twelve days ago had not seen the devastation the cancer had caused.

They must not see him like this!

The memories must be of a Champion.

How could we expect them to understand that this great Champion, this legend in his own time, was about to win his greatest victory.

The months of preparation had affected the Priest as well as Bob Tattersall.

Like every other person who had met Bob Tattersall, Father John Gaughran had been challenged and changed.

Father John had met a man like the Bible's King David, a man after God's own heart.

A man's man.

A King of his domain.

A conqueror.

A Warrior.

A winner.

A sinner.

A man with all the qualities of man, both good and bad. A man who lived life to the fullest. A hard man who drank too much, cussed too loud and brought forth every emotion known to man out into the open for all to see.

And people loved it!

They loved Bob Tattersall because he dared to be different, because he wore his emotions like a badge.

They loved him because he was honest, refusing to hide a part of himself in the closet.

What you saw was what you got.

The two men had shared life over the past months.

Soon they would share the victory over death.

Fingers clasped over the frail weak hand brought

10

back memories of that first visit and that first strong hand shake, the day when the life and the legend became a part of Father John's life.

***

The priest walked down the half-darkened marble-floored hall. The click of his heels resounded in a soft echo. His nostrils still twitched at the antiseptic smell of the hospital and his ears perked, listening for bits of conversation mixed with familiar groans and cries.

He was on familiar ground. This was his turf; his battleground. Hospital robes and soiled sheets changed people, both those who came to visit and those being cared for. Here people were glad to see you. Here they would ask the questions they were afraid to ask elsewhere.

Serving those in need included the injured, the sick and the dying.

Calming the injured brought great rewards.

Praying for the sick and seeing them recover brought great joy.

Sharing a victory over death was the ultimate satisfaction.

"John! I just met a man who thinks he's a Catholic because he went to a Catholic School."

John turned to the Chaplain, "What room is he in? I've got to meet this guy."

Bob Tattersall lay in the bed, his gauze-covered right foot hanging in a sling suspended from the apparatus bolted to the bed.

"Bob, I'm Father John Gaughran. What happened to your foot?"

Tat shook hands with the priest and began to explain the hazards of big time auto racing.

Race cars are built to go fast. Their metal and fiberglass bodies are thin and fastened to the cars in sections for quick removal. Hot fluids generated by the powerful engines escape as a fine spray which searches out the tiny cracks and crevices of the firewall and the body work. There is no floor mat or covering to protect a driver's feet and hot fluid seems to have a mind of its own when it comes to them.

The right foot must stay on the gas pedal at all times and the result of a long race is usually a boot covered with hot oil and dirt; not to mention a well cooked foot.

In the 50's and 60's race drivers wore boots or canvas shoes and heavy socks. You could tell how much racing a man had done by the grubby condition of his driving shoes.

The 100 lap race in Toronto, Canada, on June 17, 1970 had cooked Bob Tattersall's right foot, and especially his big toe, to the point a cannibal would have refused it.

The skin grafts were healing nicely.

"He doesn't like hospitals," the priest had been warned.

Hospitals were out of his element.

Nurses in white dresses gave the orders and you better not cross them.

Perhaps they reminded him of the nuns back in his school days who commanded respect from a wild kid who had been kicked out of the public schools.

After that first meeting, Father John had made it a point to get to know Bob Tattersall.

Tat, on the other hand was not ready to get friendly with a man of God. Like Simon Peter, the rough and tough fisherman from Galilee, inside he was saying, "Go away from me, for I am a sinful man."

Father John wasn't about to go away!

He made it a habit to drop by the Ligori Scrap Yard every once in a while.

When Tat would see him, he would give a big wave and keep on walking...away from the priest!

Father John would walk around like he was interested

in the operation of the car salvage business although people salvage was his true interest.

The Priest fit right into the scenery at the yard. He loved to dress in bib overalls and many times would go down to the torch pit and watch the bright shower of sparks from the cutting torch slice its way thru the mangled bodies of discarded automobiles.

This Bob Tattersall presented quite a challenge.

Just what this priest loved most!

(Left) **Bob in 1970 when Father John first met him.** *Dee Tattersall Collection.*
(Right) **Dee with Father John.** *Dee Tattersall Collection.*

Behold, I was shaped in iniquity, and in sin did my mother conceive me. Psalms 51:5

2
Youth

Robert George Tattersall came into this world with a great fuss on July 27, 1924. He was born with a veiled face, a rare occasion even in those days.

"This child is marked for greatness," his mother was told.

The membrane that formed the veil clipped away and the customary first smack on the back, given to all babies, seemed enough reason for the child to seek revenge for the next forty-seven years.

The first boy in a family with four daughters brought great joy to his English father and Scottish mother.

The birth of a second son two years later gave little Robert a playmate.

Six years later, Robert learned about death for the first time. Brother Billy was dead.

Every Saturday night during the summer there were free movies shown at the park. During intermission the kids would run across the street to the ice cream store. Robert was to look after his little brother on this night and had tried to take his hand as they prepared to cross the street.

Billy jerked his hand away. "I don't need any help," he shouted as he bolted into the street and the path of an oncoming car.

Five days later he was gone.

For a child in the second grade, the loss was devastating. Shielded from the light at birth, Robert had fought to see this new world. Now death had smacked him in the face. Life with his brother and sisters had been fun until now.

When Robert started going to school, he had to go to bed at an earlier hour and get up sooner. Billy had been his comforter from his one fear; Robert feared the dark and could not sleep alone.

He would sit on the stairs each evening and whine, "Billy, come on to bed! Billy, you don't want to stay up!" Soon, Billy would reluctantly give in and join his brother.

With the death of Billy, Robert George began to challenge death.

Life ought to be fun.

Man ought to be happy.

Rebellion set in when the young Tattersall discovered that everything fun was forbidden.

The burden of Billy's death was compounded less than a year later.

Little Kathryn idolized her brother and followed him around like a little puppy. One day Robert was trying to pry a board loose. When it wouldn't budge, he got a screwdriver and began to pound it into the board.

"Get back Kay! This screwdriver might fly up and hit you."

"No it won't."

The next hard hit with the hammer sent the instrument flying; straight into Kay's eye. While the sisters and Robert's mother rushed the injured girl to the doctor, the frightened youngster hid.

By the time they got to the doctor, the eye was gone and so was Robert George Tattersall's desire to be in authority over other people.

Not only did he rebel at being placed in charge, he refused to submit to any authority placed over him.

The young Tattersall quickly became unmanageable to the point that he was kicked out of public school.

A few days later Father Higgins, the local priest, stopped by the Tattersall home. The priest had heard about the troubled lad.

Dealing with rebellion was his line of work.

"Let us take him. We have a fine school."

Tat never forgot his father's exact words.

"I don't care where you take the sonofabitch!"

The word wasn't spread out.

It was said as one word.

For the rest of his life Tat would use the word in reference to anything he considered of little value or when he wanted to make a strong point.

He didn't use that word around Sister Mary Martina or any of the other nuns that ran his new school, and while he was on his best behavior during school hours, he seemed even wilder when he was out.

Sister Martina and Father Higgins were especially proud of the seventh grade basketball team young Robert played on.

Bob, as he liked to be called, became best friends with Francis Barsi while on the team. These two, along with the Sheedy brothers, Bob Milus and Gene Morrow, won their share of games for the all Catholic school.

Being good in basketball wasn't enough for Robert George. He always had to find a way to be the best in everything.

One such way to prove one's manhood, was to jump off the Seneca bridge into the Illinois River. Only the "fools" were brave enough for this trick and several people had committed suicide by jumping from the structure which was high enough for large ships to pass under.

The girls loved it.

Bob also joined in the escapade of placing the wagon

on top of the school. Helping the older boys with the task gave him some new friends. Bob was a small kid and the older boys took him with them and watched over him. They also like to pick up the runt and throw him around like a basketball.

His sisters watched over him too, and stood up to any who wanted to fight the small lad. Of course there was no protection when Bob was tormenting them.

He punched Eleanor once and she picked up a pop bottle and took off after him. The only room in the house with a lock was the bathroom and Bob headed for it. The door was almost shut when Eleanor got to it. She threw the pop bottle at the last moment. The sound of broken glass ended her desire to fight. Now she was in trouble.

The depression made it very hard to earn money, however, the youngster managed to acquire enough green stuff to purchase a motorcycle.

Frank Barsi, who picked up the nickname "Bucko" (a shortened version of Buckaroo) early in life, was offered one of the first rides on the cycle. Bob took him down main street which was under repair at the time as one of the government's programs during the depression.

It was the only time Bucko ever rode with his friend on a two wheeler. Once was enough!

Bob's sister, Betty Ann, still hasn't forgotten how Bob tore her new jacket to pieces when he drove through a fence while wearing it without permission.

Leora was the oldest and lived with her grandparents much of the time, but Bob got to her also. During his teen years he got into a fight with his dad and moved in with Leora and her new husband to let Dad cool off. While there, he got into the habit of borrowing the car. A couple of months later, Bob didn't come home for several days. Leora went to look for him and found the car with the motor burnt up.

Bob had moved back home. Dad wasn't mad anymore.

George Tattersall was a hard working man. He drank a bit after work and used strong language. He had a quick temper, but cooled off just as quick. When he drank he became a lover instead of getting mean like some men do. His son was like him in many ways. Like the fearful lion in "Alice in Wonderland," under all that gruff noise was a pussycat.

Once Dad threw a hammer through a storm window that wouldn't come out and exclaimed in triumph, "Now you're out!"

One time when Robert was about to get a spanking, he challenged, "You'll have to catch me first!" He made it to the Catholic school yard two blocks away before George caught him. On the return trip a boot hit him in the rear every-other step.

While the father and son seemed to fight a lot, deep inside, Robert George Tattersall was the apple of his father's eye.

There was trouble at home when the family Model A became a hot rod and Mom Tattersall was knocked off the porch while sitting in her favorite rocker. It was Tat's first car crash.

Bob was supposed to put the car into the garage, not drive it around the house.

The new motorcycle also became a wedge between father and son when the teenager ran the president of Dupont off the road. George was so mad he took a hatchet and destroyed the cycle. Bob was brave, but he wasn't about to try to take that hatchet from his Dad.

Nevertheless, running cars off the road remained a great sport for the uncontrollable teen.

While Bob was constantly into mischief, he was quite the gentleman around women. His mother was a soft, gentle person who loved good jokes and laughter. She always tried to repeat jokes but would start laughing before the punch line and could never get it right. She didn't swear and hated gossip.

Bob's love and respect for his mother carried over to the nuns at the Catholic school who taught him good manners.

If you asked Bob to do something, he would do what he could. It was "being told what to do" that he rebelled against.

The Catholic school helped him because the sisters were always polite and earned the child's respect. The experience settled the youth down enough to graduate from Secena High School.

Two months after graduating, Bob turned eighteen. Five months later he was in Uncle Sam's Army as part of the 461st Amphibious Truck Company.

Bob was in the military for three years and two days. When his unit was sent overseas in 1944, Bob had been in long enough to be fed up with Army life.

"To heck with the Army! Always some sonofabitch giving orders. It's just like school!"

ROBERT GEORGE TATTERSALL IS AWOL SIR.

Del Classen was sent by his sergeant to retrieve the AWOL Private. When Del found him, they got to having so much fun, it was two weeks before they went back.

"Let's join the paratroopers!"

"If we do that they won't court martial us," reasoned the young Private.

So Bob became a paratrooper in the United States Army.

If he wanted action, he had come to the right place. The unit saw combat in Normandy, Northern France, the Andennes Forest, the Rhineland and Central Europe.

Bob tore up his knee during his last jump into Belgium in enemy territory. A local family hid him in a flour barrel and saved his life.

He was later captured but only spent a few weeks as a prisoner of war.

A short time later the conflict was over.

He didn't tell anyone he was being discharged on December 4, 1945 and when he arrived home unannounced his mother almost had a heart attack.

Bob never talked much about his Army days or his medals. There was a job to do during the war and he came home a changed man, ready to get on with life.

He liked to joke about getting the "Good Conduct Medal" after being AWOL. The Purple Heart, American Campaign, the Victory and European-Middle-Eastern with silver star rounded out the collection.

When Bob got out of the army, he went to work at Dupont, the dynamite factory where his father worked.

Motorcycles were his main mode of transportation and maintaining them expensive. Many a night he would pull into a closed gas station and take down the pump hoses, draining the last ounce of the precious fuel into a special container he carried.

With enough fuel to get to the next station, off he'd go, working his way back home.

Bigger money could be made with the Chicago Bridge & Steel Company. Working the high iron was a dangerous job and the men were among the toughest on earth. Hard work, flirting with death every day, led to hard drinking and wild women at night.

Going around once and grabbing all the gusto you can get became the byword of Tat's life.

Chicago Bridge & Steel was a good paying job but required long hours and lots of work. It sure didn't leave much room for fun.

Truck driving was more up Tat's alley. It became a useful way to make money and also have the freedom to go racing.

His first trucking venture with a local young man was short-lived. Bob awoke one night while in the sleeper. The truck, with the young partner driving, was moving way too fast down a mountain road.

"What's going on?" shouted a wide-awake rider.

"We lost the brakes," came the reply.

"Ditch it!" shouted Tat.

The youth froze as the ex-paratrooper leaped from the sleeper. Steering the rig into a tree-lined ditch ended the partnership.

Bob loved cowboy clothes and western movies were his favorite during the free shows. While trucking out west he bought cowboy souvenirs for those back home.

Bob's father had raced in his younger years in the "Silver Streak" he had built. He had introduced his son to racing by taking him to the track many times as he was growing up.

Stock car and midget racing flourished right after the war and Bob told himself, "I can do that!"

Getting paid to run over people, shoving cars out of the way and out-braving others fit Bob Tattersall like hand and glove.

(Top) Bob's 1935 6th grade class. Bob is 5th from the right in the center row. *Dee Tattersall Collection.*

(Center Left) Robert did not jump from the roadway, he climbed to the top of the structure and jumped into the Illinois River. *Ed Watson photo.*

(Center Right) The Catholic School at Seneca. *Ed Watson photo.*

(Below) Bob Tattersall *left* with Robert Roney on the Seneca Bridge the year Bob jumped into the Illinois River. *Dee Tattersall Collection.*

(Left) **Private Robert Tattersall.** *Dee Tattersall Collection.*
(Top Right) **A good reason to go AWOL?** *Dee Tattersall Collection.*
(Lower Right) **Bob just after the war with his cycle.** *Dee Tattersall Collection.*

Ponder the path of thy feet, and let all thy ways be established. Proverbs 4:26.

3

UARA

The renewal of the running of the Indianapolis 500 Mile Race in 1946 helped place auto racing in the public eye.

People were hungry for entertainment; anything with action.

Midget auto racing had been around before the war. With the troops coming home and the shortage of automobiles (because the factories had not had time to convert to peacetime production) stock car racing got off to a slower start than the midgets. Passenger cars that weren't running had been cut up and melted down to make tanks.

Midget racing, on the other hand, had cars ready to run and the specially constructed machines were easy to build and maintain.

Production of new cars didn't get going until 1946 and the waiting list for new cars was long. The economy was booming. People trading in their old Fords provided midget racing with the now famous V8/60 engine which became the staple of the sport for several years.

By 1947 midget racing had invaded the country. Ray Elliott was declared the area midget champion that year and in 1948 the United Auto Racing Association was formed in Joliet, Illinois. Elliott won again in 1948 and

49. He was on his way to his third UARA Championship and his fourth area crown in 1950 when twenty-six year old Bob Tattersall came to the South Bend, Indiana Speedway to take his first ride in a midget race car.

Art Ross was the owner and Willy's was the power.

To those who never sat in a midget race car it is hard to explain the tremendous sensations the small cars produce.

Imagine sitting in an office chair with arms on it. The back and sides are covered with thick padded leather upholstery so that when you sit down you are packed into the seat.

The chair legs have been shortened so that your knees are level with your waist. The floor is flat in the center, but makes a ninety degree curved bend to form the bellypan. The left foot sets loose. The right one rests in a horseshoe shaped cup to keep your foot in one place. The accelerator looks like an upside down spoon and feels like it will go through the floor if you spit on it. Learning the "feel" of it will take practice.

The steering assembly is shaped like an inverted "T." The steering wheel is attached to the shaft of the T and the cross shaft has been padded because it touches your knees.

When you reach your hands out at a 45 degree angle you can take hold of the tires and move the vehicle much like wheelchair patients do.

A mere five feet in front of you is the nose of the car giving you an open view of the roadway ahead.

Between your legs is the gear box, called an in-and-out clutch. Picture a doughnut with teeth inside the hole. Now picture your finger with matching teeth protruding upward. When you slide the doughnut over your finger the teeth interlock and the doughnut cannot rotate unless your finger does.

When you push down on the clutch lever a gear slides

forward over the opposing gear bolted into the back of the crank shaft. The car is either in gear or out of gear. The drive shaft running from the engine through the clutch, between your legs and under your seat, is turning 6,000 rpms when the engine is turning 6,000 rpms. Imagine running up to 100 miles per hour in your chair.

Now you have a sense of what an 800 pound midget race car is like.

That is what Bob Tattersall, along with hundreds of other men, fell in love with.

The unique well-balanced package of explosive power that made you feel like you and the car were one unit, were called "Buzz Bombs" for good reason.

Tat would continue to race stock cars for awhile, but after that first midget ride, he would never be the same.

When a midget and its driver become one it is like roller skating when the skates become your feet.

Midgets have a quick response. You could get a car sideways and almost pick it up and turn it back in the right direction by raising up in the seat. They also turned upside down with ease should the tires dig into the track at just the right angle or you rode up over the exposed wheels of another car.

In one of Tat's first races he ran up over Ray Elliott's hood.

"Ain't this fun!" he exclaimed.

"You can't tip these things."

Bob Tattersall would get upside down some twenty-nine times in a midget race car during his career.

If stock cars allowed Tat to bully his way, pushing and shoving to gain position, midgets required new tactics, at least that's what everybody thought.

Tat seemed to have a different idea.

You could still push and shove with a midget, you just had to be more precise.

He deducted that the easiest way to pass in midget

racing was to start on the outside of a corner and instead of following the other cars, just make a straight line for the lowest point in the turn. When you came out into traffic on the other side you just had to be careful where you touched the other driver. If your tire got behind the other driver's tire, the forward rotation of his wheel would pick your right front wheel up causing the left front tire to dig in.

Next thing you'd know, your car would be rolling sideways down the track.

On the other hand, if your tires touched side to side you simply bounced off each other.

Bob Tattersall learned how to bounce off.

He also learned another, safer trick.

How to place a car up against the fence and power by on the outside.

Bob Tattersall had entered the sport of midget auto racing at a time in history when it would be the biggest training ground for drivers at Indianapolis.

For the next fifteen years, midget drivers would dominate the 500 Mile Race fields.

Bob Tattersall would not be among them, yet Indy's greatest who raced against him or saw him race would be heard to say that he was the best when it came to driving a midget race car.

(Top) Tat #12 Coming Thru! #3 ...Wright, #10 Steve Orme, #25 Pete Peterson, #9 Allen Heath. *Bob Sheldon photo.*
(Below) #10 Ralph Stuber. #38 Bob Tattersall at the 87th St. Speedway Chicago 1954. *Bob Sheldon Photo.*

(Top) Mazon Fair 1953. #1 Tat, #3 Norm Legner, #38 Willie Wildhaber, #25 Sonny Bessett, #10 Ralph Stuber. *Dee Tattersall Collection.*
(Left) 1962 Tat in Paul Baines Offy #3 Johnny Riva #73. *Ed Hitze photo.*
(Right) Tat tries to drive thru Bud Williams during a Cincinnati, Ohio Indoor Race in 1953. *Dee Tattersall Collection.*
(Below) "No You Don't," Tat screams at Willie. Tat #57, Willie in the Pavese #27 at Kankakee, Illinois in 1958. *Dee Tattersall Collection.*

And the Lord God said, It is not good that the man should be alone; I will make him a helper fit for him. Genesis 2:18.

4

Dee

Her name is Delores, but don't you call her that. Delores was the name Tat used when he meant business.

Everyone calls her Dee.

Bob Tattersall was eight years old when Frank and Jeanette Ligori became the proud parents of their third child.

It was 1932 and the effects of the great depression were still being felt in Streator, Illinois, the "Glass Container Capitol" of the world.

The used car parts business behind the Ligori home allowed Frank to be an able provider for his family.

From the beginning Dee needed to be where the action was. She hung close to her thirteen month older brother, Clifford, rather than her sisters, Jean and Betty.

A tomboy, Dee liked to beat up on both boys and girls. Cliff and her other brother, Jim, gave her many chances.

Later when young Mickey was born into the family, it was Dee who looked after him.

Dee was 13 when World War II ended and life was simple around the wrecking yard located on the north side of Streator. Next door a tavern had been built, and behind the tavern was the quarter mile Streator Speedway.

There was constant traffic in and out; the wrecking yard by day, the tavern by night, and the speedway on weekends. Something exciting was happening all the time.

Even going to church was exciting. Frank was Catholic and Jeanette a Methodist. It was Grandma who took command of the spiritual upbringing as she alternated each week between the two churches.

When Dee was thirteen her dad said she was old enough to decide for herself.

She did decide. Seven years later; after she was married to Bob Tattersall she chose to be baptized into the Methodist Church.

Dee had no idea in those early years that God had special plans for her.

She would not become the woman behind a successful man. No, for Bob Tattersall much more was required.

Tat's woman would have to be a companion, a friend, a buddy, a lover, a chauffeur and someone as strong willed as he was.

Tat's woman could not survive walking behind him. She would have to walk beside him, and the two would truly have to become one.

The woman who married Bob Tattersall would have to be one of the most loving, forgiving, and understanding women God ever made.

Love isn't "Never having to say you're sorry!"

Love is "knowing the worst about a person and loving them in spite of it!"

Of course, Dee didn't know she was all these things. She merely thought she was the toughest girl in all of Illinois.

The tavern provided plenty of action for a tough young woman, and of course, the racers had to have a drink after eating dust from the dirt track all night.

One of the midget drivers had taken a liking to Dee and she to him.

Willie Wildhaber, driving for Bill Ross, was rightly named! He was one of the top chauffeurs in that part of the world and the crowds loved his hard driving. They called him, "Wild Willie."

Dee had watched the races looking over the fence while perched atop one of the cars in the wrecking yard.

Now that she was eighteen she could visit the tavern and spend time with Willie.

One night Willie came into the establishment with a new guy. He was a handsome devil with a short crew cut and squared-off jaw. He didn't seem to have a lot of muscle, but the looks were deceiving.

Tomboy, Dee, found out the hard way!

"Dee, this is Bob Tattersall."

The next thing you know, they had become a three-some, Dee dating both guys and many nights all three running around together.

One night Willie and Tat smacked a car that was stopped in the road. Both, a bit drunk, jumped out of the car and tried to convince the guy it was his fault for stopping.

He wanted them to go to the police station and Willie said, "There's no need for both of us going. I'll ride with you."

Tat took off and went home to Seneca.

When Willie and the man got to the police station they wanted to know, "Who was the other driver?"

Willie said, "I don't know! I was a hitchhiker and he just picked me up."

The next morning a cop car was at the Tattersall residence in Seneca.

Willie was at Dee's, asking her to take a ride to Ottawa with him.

"Sure."

When they got to town Willie asked Dee, "Have you got thirty-five dollars?"

"Yup."

Dee gave Willie the money and he dashed off upstairs.

He was only gone a few minutes and then drove Dee back home.

Half-an-hour later here comes old Tattersall.

"Wanta take a ride to Ottawa?"

"OK."

When they got to town, here came the question.

"Have you got thirty-five dollars?"

The two connivers had each gotten thirty-five dollars from Dee, paid their fines, and driven her back home.

Neither of them had a date with her that night. In fact, they weren't seen in Streator for several days.

***

Jeanette Ligori, like her daughter, is a remarkable woman. She must know thousands of stories about Tat, but when asked to tell the juicy tales, she remarks, "He never said anything bad about me, and I'm not saying anything bad about him."

Mom does tell about a time her husband acquired a beautiful Model A.

"What's wrong with it? Gotta be something wrong. We don't get cars like that here."

Frank told her, "It has a bit of a fish smell. The guy that had it used it for a fishing car before he died."

Tattersall could not wait to try out the little Model A, smell or no smell.

The car was so pretty that the neighbor, Mr. Lenhausen, came out to admire it. He was standing in front of it when Tat fired up the engine and without warning jammed his foot to the floor.

Mr. Lenhausen dove into the dirt to keep from being

run over.

Moments later the Ligori phone rang.

"Your daughter and that guy she goes with just about killed Peter!"

It was Mrs. Lenhausen, who would end up being Tat's nurse when he was dying. Like most who met him, she came to love him.

The family did take the car to Fairbury for the races after that. The smell from old bait and dead fish made everybody sick on the way home.

**

One morning when Dee got up her mother had some bad news.

"I think your boyfriend got killed last night. His motorcycle is up at the corner with the front wheel off and his boots are strewed all over. The saddle bags are torn and there's clothing all the way up Bloomington Street."

Getting a flat tire at high speed when you're drunk will do that sort of thing.

DEATH, YOU'LL HAVE TO WAIT.

Sister Mary Martina is praying for Bob.

You'll try the crash routine again and again. Each time you'll fail.

**

It was May of 1950 when Bob Tattersall walked into the tavern with Wild Willie.

Six months later, on November 13, 1950, in front of a Justice of the Peace, Delores Ligori took the vows she would live with for the next twenty-one years.

While Dee was taking her vows, Bob Tattersall was acquiring what he called, "His own private stock," and the best wife in all of Illinois.

(Top Right) Bob and Dee in 1951.

(Top Left) Dee as a teenager. *Dee Tattersall Collection.*

(Below) The life of a driver's wife. Dee waits patiently behind the autograph seekers. *Wayne Bryant photo.*

"Set me as a seal upon thine heart, as a seal upon thine arm; for love is strong as death." Song of Solomon 8:6.

5
Young Married

Getting married in the winter was God's timing. The young couple had the opportunity to set the pattern for their life together before racing season began.

Tat was driving semis and scavenging the parts yard for the makings of a great stock car.

"This is great!" thought Tat.

He had a new wife, a new home in Streator (complements of Dee's brother) and all the supplies he'd ever need for his expensive racing habit.

One night he decided he wanted to go downtown and drink with the boys.

"Fine," was Dee's reply, "but you better be home by midnight. Any later and I won't be here."

"I'll be back by midnight, Dee," Tat assured her.

"OK. But if you're not, I won't be here."

Midnight came, and no Tattersall.

An hour later Dee heard the car door and that familiar whistle.

Tat would always whistle at the door and Dee would repeat the notes.

This time, no answer.

The well-lit husband came into the house.

No Dee!

Not in the bedroom either!

Dee had hidden under the bed at the first sound of his

arrival.

She saw his feet come within inches of her nose.

Flop!

The steel cross members touched her back as he sat down on the bed.

His feet shifted as he stood up.

His pants fell in a heap around his ankles.

Flop!

Hands fumbled with the pants before removing the shoes so he could lift his feet from them.

He fell back on the bed.

The feet shifted again as he stood to remove his shirt.

At that moment Dee grabbed his ankles.

"Woaaaa."

Two feet sprang off the floor.

Flop!

The next thing Dee knew, Tat was standing up in the bed jumping up and down as hard as he could shouting, "Come out of there you sonofabitch! Come out!"

The big coil springs bounced and the steel cross bars dug into Dee's back, who was laughing so hard she could not have come out if the house was on fire.

"You crazy sonofabitch. I could have cut you to ribbons," a more sober and younger Tat told his wife when he had her in his arms. "Took ten years off my life."

Bob Tattersall was a sexy husband and he was a good lover.

Making love was like drinking; He'd do it all the time if he didn't have to work.

When Dee wasn't in the mood, or Bob was a little too inebriated, Dee would run out of the house, with Bob right behind her, chasing his woman.

Once Dee ran around the house a couple of times then spotted a car with the front end removed. She jumped under the front fender and from her crouched position watched Bob run by lap after lap until he went back into the house.

Twenty minutes later she returned and found her husband sound asleep.

He would remember nothing in the morning.

The next morning was always a new start for Tat. He woke up sober, ready to go to work, and seldom looked back. The challenge of today loomed ahead. Time to go out and spit in life's eye.

The young couple's first anniversary became a wild affair not soon to be forgotten.

When the Tattersalls went drinking, it was always Dee who became the designated driver.

Someone had to drive Tat home.

They had gone to Ottawa to celebrate. Tat had a loaded semi trailer to deliver, and was drinking lightly. Dee, on the other hand was enjoying the party.

When another group in the tavern began throwing bottles, Dee and Bob thought it was a good time to leave.

The tavern owner had called the law. "Everyone stay where you are," he bellowed.

"I've got a load to deliver," Tat told him.

"I don't care what you got! Stick around."

Moments later a city cop appeared on the scene.

"I've got a load to deliver."

"Look, nothing's going to happen to you. You weren't involved. Just stick around until the deputy sheriff gets here."

That's when Dee's mouth began to be driven by the liquor that had flowed through it.

"Shut up Dee!"

"I won't. They don't have a right to keep us."

The deputy placed the bottle throwers in one car.

Dee and Tat occupied the other.

"You remind me of Gannon and Friday. A couple of Dragnet cops. We didn't have anything to do with it."

"Tell it to the sheriff lady!"

The sheriff wasn't there when they got to the jail and had to be called.

When he arrived he said, "I don't want to hear it. Tell it to the judge."

By the time the judge got there Dee's dad had arrived to bail them out.

"Dee, keep your mouth shut."

Too late! She's already mad.

The judge ordered, "Come in here."

Dee just sat there.

Dad kicked her. "Get in there."

"No, my name's Delores and he can address me that way."

Finally she went before the judge who asked her, "What happened?"

"The city cop said to tell it to the deputy. The deputy said to tell it to the sheriff. The sheriff said tell it to the judge. To heck with you all. I'm going to tell it to the Marine Corps."

"LOCK HER UP!"

They did. Tat was taken in one direction and Dee in the other.

"I need a smoke. I'm a gooddamn tax paper. Bring me a cigarette."

The turnkey would no sooner get downstairs and he'd hear.

"I have to go to the toilet."

She could have squeezed thru the bars, she was so skinny.

"You're getting deeper and deeper."

Finally Dad had convinced the judge that Dee really hadn't done any bottle throwing and only needed to be taken home and allowed to sleep it off.

He had signed the papers, but when Dee saw them she thought they said the fine was $3500. Her eyes couldn't read the decimal point. The figure was $35.00.

"My dad can't afford that. You can just lock me back up again because my dad ain't paying it."

"Will you shut up Dee and sign the paper!"

"Where's Bob?"

"I'm not getting him out! He's the one that got you into all this."

"No, daddy, It was my fault. Get Bob out here or I'm going back."

The three left Ottawa in a hurry. Frank Ligori was $70 lighter than when he arrived.

***

The life style for this couple was simple. Work hard by day, drink and play hard at night. The pattern was set.

Dave Booth summed it up best.

"Tat made an impression wherever he went. He was "loud" and you certainly knew he was around."[1]

In doing this book and conducting interviews I would constantly hear, "I know a good story, but you can't print it."

***

Dee knew about the other women.

At first it hurt deeply. Later, it would only be a sore spot.

Tat's "other women" in Australia was to be expected, reasoned Dee. After all, he was gone for four months at a time.

One thing was always clear; Tat liked women, but he loved Dee.

"Sure I was mad, but I was happier with him than I could ever have been without him."

"I loved him! God, I dearly loved him. The women hurt, but he always came home. I felt that divorce was worse than death, especially if you loved somebody as much as I loved him. He did what he wanted to do, but he always came home. And he had no reason to come home if he didn't love me, we had no kids, I wasn't working and he wasn't going to inherit any millions. He didn't have any special girl friend; just a lot of them. Just mix them up. What the heck. Just wanted to use them for awhile."

What hurt more was when so called friends would drive local girls to the track for Bob.

One night two such "friends" delivered one to South Bend, Indiana.

Dee had told Tat she wasn't going to go to the races that weekend.

"You'll have to get someone else to chauffeur you, I'm not going."

When Dee didn't go Tat would tell everyone she was sick.

"Dee don't feel good. Dee didn't want to come."

That afternoon Dee told her mom, "Think I'll jump in the car and go to South Bend."

"Why?"

"I think the girl from Streator is there."

Sure as life, there she was.

Dee left her car at South Bend and rode with Tat the remainder of the weekend. They fought all the way.

"There's nothing to it Dee," he assured her. "You know there's nothing to it. Just fun."

It irritated Dee that after going through the lean years, when he had a few bucks in his pocket, he'd blow it on other women.

Years later the same woman came up again.

Dee had passed a local tavern and Bob's semi was parked out front. When she got home she called the tavern.

"I thought you were on your way to Peoria?"

"I'm leaving right now!"

Dee circled back uptown and the truck was still there. She was pretty sure who the girl was and drove by her house.

Sure enough, the car was gone.

Dee lay in wait.

Before long, here they came. Dee got right up behind them and laid on the horn.

The girl took off with Dee right on her tail. Off they went hither and yon, over curbs and berms; the whole bit. Dee gave them a merry chase.

When the girl pulled up in front of Tat's semi, Dee had her by the hair before she could get out of the car.

She yanked and looked down to see what looked like a head in her fist.

"God! I've pulled her head off!"

Not knowing she had on a wig, Dee thought she had decapitated the girl.

While they were out there fist fighting in the middle of the street, Bob climbed into his semi, started the engine and shouted.

"I ain't got time to mess with you sonofabitches. I got to take this load to Peoria!"

And he drove off, leaving the two women in the middle of the street.

When he came home the next day he told Dee, "There's nothing to it. There's just nothing to it. Just Fun."

(*Above*) L to R. Dale Pierce, Willie Wildhaber, Tat, Dee, Judy Pierce. *Dee Tattersall Collection.*
(*Center*) Bob and Dee at Daytona Beach 1957. *Dee Tattersall Collection.*
(*Below Left*) Bob and Dee, 1951. *Dee Tattersall Collection.*
(*Below Right*) Bob and Dee's Second Anniversary, 1952. *Dee Tattersall Collection.*

(*Top Left*) **Dee does the Hula.**
Dee Tattersall Collection.
(*Top Right*) **Betty Hancock and Tat.**
Dee Tattersall Collection.
(*Right*) **Bob and Dee Feb. 3, 1960.**
Dee Tattersall Collection.
(*Below Left*) **The Captain of the
Oriana greets the Tattersalls for the
1960 cruise.** *Dee Tattersall Collection.*
(*Below Right*) **Tat still chasing Dee,
Australia, 1960.** *Dee Tattersall Collection.*

Willie Wildhaber. Joliet Stadium. 1959. *Dee Tattersall Collection.*

For man looketh on the outward appearance, but the Lord looketh on the heart. I Samuel 16:7.

6

Mr. Nice

The trucking business was good in the early 50's. Tat was driving long hauls to Texas for Consolidated Freight Lines and short hauls for Gould and Talbot.

Dee made many of the short trips with her husband to St. Louis or Milwaukee on the two lane highways that covered the land.

Willie was also trucking and would send cards to his two favorite people.

One said, "Don't know what to tell you."

It was signed, Willie, and addressed to Robert Tattersall, Streator, Illinois, % Gould and Talbot Frucking Co.

Another said, "Here's your post card. Can't say I don't remember you. Wish you were here. They were expecting you yesterday. They had real guns too. No sense of humor." It was signed: Mr. Wildhaber to you.

One day Frank Ligori sent Tat to Joliet to pick up two jeeps he had purchased. Tat took young Mickey with him.

Late in the day, when they didn't come back, Dee and her mom went looking for them. They found the pair in the Brass Rail in Ottawa.

Mickey, who was not even a teenager, was sitting on the bar with a shot glass of Coke and Tat was loaded.

To top it all off, they only had one jeep. Tat hoped to repeat the adventure again the next day.

However, it was Mickey that caught the dickens from Mom. "Mitchell Lee Ligori, you know how to drive. You should have come home."

***

Once, when Tat was driving the semi home down route 23, he spotted Jack Feken stopped at a crossroads. Jack wanted to turn right onto the busy highway but his view was blocked by a parked tractor trailer.

Tat stopped his truck in the middle of the highway and jumped out. Stopping traffic, he waved the Streator native on and then jumped back into his rig and headed home.

He was always doing silly little things like that and people enjoyed the skinny man with the big personality.

To most people Bob Tattersall was Mr. Nice. To the fans he was the greatest. The complex person inhabiting that tall, ruddy complected frame, could get under your skin, but somehow you came away liking the guy.

Driving semis is a lonely job. The long hours on the road without company was a good living. "I'm my own boss," he would tell people. Still, there was a constant need for companionship. Deep inside he needed to be liked and he worked at making friends.

Tat remembered his childhood days and went out of

his way when it came to youth.

The kids at the Quarter Midget track at 113th and route 47 loved it when Willie and Tat would stop by and help Jim Cushing handle the kids. Larry Brooks remembers it as if it were yesterday. "It was quite a thrill to perform before real race drivers."

Randy Lewis was only twelve years old in 1957 but he remembers the checkered flags given out by the Wynn's Oil Company. The feature winner would be given the flag to make a victory lap at Joliet. Most drivers would throw the flag into the stands causing a mad scramble. Tat began the practice of stopping the car after the victory lap, then walking to the stands he would present it to a child.

Randy wanted one so badly that he wrote to Dee. The next week Bob won the feature and walked over to give the flag to the Streator youth, however, the boy next to him snatched it away.

The next week Tat won again and this time he made sure Randy got it.

Pat Casey was a speech handicapped youth who never missed a race. He too received a checkered flag handed to him personally so he would not get hurt by the crowd of children.

When Pat was sent to a special training school many miles from home he received a card every week from his idol. The cards were placed in his special scrapbook titled, "My Family."

Rhonda Crawford was only ten when Tat brought Jack Stroud's midget to the Streator School and gave a talk on safe driving. Rhonda relates that the talk worked. She's only had one wreck, which was not her fault.

His old friend, "Hacksaw" remembers stopping by the garage when he first met Tat. Tat was working on an engine and Hacksaw was standing by the end of the work table. Every time Tat would walk by he would say, "Excuse me." The local native had never seen a man be so courteous while at work.

Because of his size as a youth, Tat had learned to use words effectively. Many a battle had been won by knowing when to shout and when to run. Since Tat didn't like running, he became quite proficient at using his vocabulary, usually at high volume. He knew how and when to be charming and put such knowledge to good use.

His philosophy for racing was expressed one night at the "National Speedcar Club" in Sydney. "Never put yourselves ahead of the public's interests," he instructed as he told them how American racing had declined.

The avenue to a full time racing career in the 50's was to do well in midgets at the local level, then progress to an AAA midget ride and hope for a shot at Indianapolis or at least a good sprint car.

Australia had racing clubs in the major cities. America had racing clubs in various areas. Occasionally several drivers from one club would come to race in another area.

Six St. Louis area drivers decided to invade Joliet one Saturday night. At the drivers meeting it was announced that the shrubs outside of turn four were taking a beating and any driver who drove through them would be set down for the night. During warmups Danny Burke and Tat collided and both men mauled the shrubbery. Burke was put on the trailer, and when Tat was allowed to run, Bud Hoppe, Dick Ward and Joe Finley were furious. The SLARA crew vowed they would never run UARA again.

Protecting the home team was a way of life in the different organizations. Such an attitude did not hamper Bob Tattersall. As early as 1952 Bob was racing all over and winning.

He not only won races, he also made friends. Paul

Baines remembers the first time he met Bob Tattersall. It was 1952 and they were at Hawkey Downs in Cedar Rapids, Iowa. Paul's engine let go and he shopped for a ride. Bob had towed Dale Pierce's #38 and Al Huth's #88 to the Iowa races.

"I've got two cars," said Tat. You can drive one of them."

Tat was first with Paul second that afternoon. The next day at Keokuk Paul won with Tat second.

Such friendship paid off as Paul Baines "Mattoon Imperial Motors Offy" became a top USAC ride for Tat as well as one of his Australian cars.

There was a time to be serious and a time to have fun. To Tat, having fun meant BEING LOUD.

Tat was loud at other times too.

Dave Stickland remembers Tat telling him to make a lot of noise when he went to the pay window. "The noisy gear gets the grease."

Erwin Burris learned about Tat's pay window antics at Columbus, Indiana. The race had been rained out and Burris was a new car owner with USAC, having purchased Ed Hitze's beautiful machine.

Because Erwin was a car owner and had sent in a pre-entry, he was given $50.00.

Tat got upset because the drivers didn't get paid a dime, so for several races he berated the newcomer.

One time at Eldora, on a night when several of the Speedway Mechanics were on hand, the young Burris was having trouble. When Clint Brawner, Herb Porter and Bobby Grim jumped in to help him make the race, Tat started hollering at the youngster, "You'll never have enough money to hire these guys and they're helping you for free."

Burris learned to pit as far away from Tat as he could. Yet when the midgets traveled to the dangerous high banks at Winchester, Indiana, it was Tat who brought

Chuck Rodee with him to advise the new kid on how to drive the banks.

***

Frank Welch was flagging a midget race at Mazon in the days when you took two qualifying laps, came in and then took a single lap during the second round.

When Tat had completed his first two laps he complained to Frank that he couldn't see the flags.

On the second round Frank walked to the middle of the track. With Tat coming full bore down the chute, Welch unfurled the flag and remained in the center of the track. As Tat zoomed by, Frank laid the flag across his helmet.

Tat slid sideways down into the first turn and was out of the car almost before it stopped.

With three men holding him back from Welch's throat, Frank, with a big grin on his face, asked, "Did you see the flag Tat?"

The races at Mazon were never boring and many memories of those days remain, among them were Tat and Bud Abraham taking turns in the dunk tank to raise money for an injured teen.

Many remember the girlie shows at the Mazon Fair. Once, after the main show was over the girls offered to really show them how to do it for an extra dollar. Tat shouted, "I want to see you do it in the back of a stock car at eighty miles an hour." The place went crazy, the girls ran, and the show was over.

Then there was the time the tent came down on the rowdy group, however, nothing came of it when the police realized that most of the crowd were racers.

The best time was when Dee went to the back of the tent and peeked through a hole. While she was trying to see what Tat was doing, a cop walked up and smacked her bottom with a flashlight.

Joe Shaheen thought the world of Tat, especially after Tat bothered to write a thank you letter to the Springfield promoter for the way he received the touring fans from Australia.

Ted Bohlander remembers one race where a haywagon was brought out on the main straightaway during intermission and Tat and Parnelli Jones danced to the country music.

Tat was a great dancer, and with his beautiful smile and charm was a hit with the ladies as well as the fans. Some stories written about the legend paint a picture of a crude, vulgar man and I am sure that in certain situations the stories are true. A lone woman in a bar, dressed as an open invitation, might spark such a response. To most women, Bob was charming, polite and desirable, a man who knew how to treat a lady.

To many, the complex Bob Tattersall was a man from out of the past. He would have fit right in with Barney Oldfield, Ray Harroun or the Chevrolet Brothers.

In the years he raced, men went from driving in tee shirts to Nomex uniforms, from skinny tires without roll bars to wide wheels and cages. In a world perceived as wild, Bob Tattersall would be considered the wildest.

(Top) Tat and Tony Saylor racing quarter midgets. *Dee Tattersall Collection.*
(Below) Tat giving the victory flag to the kids. *Dee Tattersall Collection.*

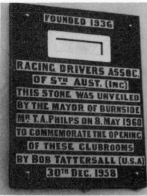

(Top) The Australian Racing Drivers Association Clubrooms. *David Brock photo*
(Left) "I'm going to tell Dee what you said." That's Reckless the USAC Clown coming to aid the girl. *Dee Tattersall Collection.*
(Right) Bob with his niece Roxanne. Aug. 8, 1959. *Dee Tattersall Collection.*
(Bottom) Tat winning at Joliet in 1958. *Dee Tattersall Collection.*

(Top Left) Bob Tattersall in 1951. *(Top Right)* Tat and young Mickey.
Dee Tattersall Collection.
(Center Left) The B-29 in 1951. *(Center Right)* Tat in the Elio Negrelli #13.
Bob Sheldon photo.
(Below Left) Ain't this fun! *Dwight Vaccaro photo.*
(Below Right) Relax, I've done this before. *Earl's racing photos.*

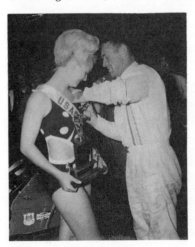

And behold, I am with thee, and will keep thee in all the places to which thou goest. Genesis 28:15.

7
Making a Legend

Legends aren't made over night, nor are great race drivers. They develop one race at a time. Legends begin within the inner circle. Reporters searching for the good stories produce the legend as the special events unfold.

Bob Tattersall and his 1937 Ford Coupe was news.

When Frank Ligori purchased an engine from the Grancor Speed Shop run by the Granatelli Brothers and helped Bob install it into his B-29 stock car, Tat found himself in the hottest stocker around.

While few remember Tat as a stock car driver, he was still racing them as late as 1956 when he won the O'Hare Mid-season Stock Car Race. He also won the first midget race run on the new speedway located south of the famous Chicago Airport.

One season at Mazon, Illinois, Tat won 27 of 29 features with his stocker. He was so good that one night two other drivers ganged up and ran him off the track.

A winning record made people know he was a good race driver.

It was the special races that made this good race driver a legend, and the special races started early.

Crashes are always good for print. If the crash is really spectacular it can get more print than winning the feature.

Early crashes in midgets got Bob Tattersall lots of

print. Learning to bump wheels with precision takes practice.

One night at Joliet Stadium, Tat took one of his memorable flips. Dee, rushing from the stands to get to her husband, scraped her bottom on the cement wall as she slipped under the protective railing.

They loaded Tat into the ambulance with Dee right by his side. When they got to the hospital Tat said he was OK, "There's nothing wrong with me."

Dee then spoke up, "Could someone take a look at my butt? I think I hurt it."

***

Tat became a hero to the racers at Charleston, Illinois. The race was an open competition affair which meant the promoter did not use a racing association to provide cars and did not have to pay the purse up front.

This promoter decided not to pay anybody. As the feature race was finishing he slipped out of the race track.

Paul Baines who drove for Tat in Iowa was a policeman in Charleston and was at the track.

Tat had won the feature in Tony Saylor's Offy. When he got word that the promoter had been seen leaving the fairgrounds Tat got mad. Seeing Paul, Tat hollered, "The promoter ducked out on us!"

"Let's go get him," shouted Baines.

They jumped into the police car and began the pursuit.

"How do we know which way he went, Tat?"

"The stealing sonofabitch doesn't think anyone will chase him. He's on his way home."

When they caught the thief near Terre Haute, Indiana, they confiscated his money, his briefcase and his typewriter.

The promoter had to follow them back to town.

With the wives in a local restaurant, the men tried to figure out a payoff at the police station.

Charges were not filed, but the word was out about this promoter.

***

No one who was there can ever forget the spin into the maintenance building at Joliet.

The cinder quarter mile track around a football field was the home of the United Auto Racing Association. Housed in a stadium with cement stands on both sides, the facility was beautified by a carpet of grass covering everything but the track.

Turns one and two had yards of grass. Turns three and four had a maintenance building some thirty yards away from the racing surface.

The pits were an extension of the main straightaway off turn four. With a large field of cars, many had to pit on the grass behind the building which set back from the middle of the turn.

The building was the size of a three car garage and had an overhead door which faced the track, and was left open.

At the start of the feature, Tat got caught in traffic on the outside; the worst place to be on the flat cinder surface. Nevertheless, Tattersall was charging going into turn three side by side with another car.

When their wheels bumped, Tat's car spun sideways and then slid backwards on the grass directly into the building.

Tat had his foot to the floor, spinning the wheels on the slick grass.

When the car hit the cement floor of the building the backward motion stopped and the sounds of squealing tires pierced the air as the building filled with blue smoke!

The car shot out of the building as if fired from a cannon.

Charging down the front stretch a half a lap behind the entire field roared one mad cowboy!

Passing cars was easy now. The field had strung out. Bob Tattersall, the "Streator Streak" went on to win the feature race.

***

In the early days of racing at Joliet, there was a flag pole at the south end of the track.

One night during a series of flips on the start of the feature, Tat's car landed way up on the flag pole before sliding down.

The height record stood for several years until Walt Wieneke of Libertyville, Illinois broke it.

The flag pole was then removed.

***

Most people have forgotten the race which didn't get the headlines because it would have embarrassed some big name drivers. The race was recorded in Speed Sport News by ace reporter, Gene Powlen.

Terre Haute, Indiana became famous among racing people because Tony Hulman, the owner of the Indianapolis Motor Speedway, made his home there.

In 1953 the half-mile dirt track at the fairgrounds was added to Terre Haute's fame. The track became known as the "Action Track" because it produced many exciting races.

It was considered mainly a sprint car track, however, the midgets were part of its history from its third year of operation.

In 1954 "Iron" Duke Nalon, who drove the Novi at Indy, won the last race of his career there, a 200 lap midget race.

Tony Bettenhausen, "The Tinley Park Express," also won in the midgets at the Action Track in 1955 and '56.

It was on the day Tony won the first race that Bob Tattersall made more racing history.

The date was October 9, 1955. Bob was still an outlaw that year, however, he felt it was time to try the big boys.

Terre Haute was a bastion of AAA racing. The race fields always contained stars who had driven in the Indianapolis 500. It was policy to allow the little guys in and the "Hut" drew large fields for its races because everyone wanted to race there.

There was little concern over the outlaw king, Bob Tattersall, when he showed up that day. After all, he had a Ford 60 engine in his car and this track was a power track; besides, who could beat the best in the business? Even if it was the fastest V8 60 in the world, it was still no match for the Offy.

On this day Frank Pavese had installed a two speed rear end in the famous car. This addition provided the equivalent of a passing gear and was used by Rodger Ward in an Offy midget at Lime Rock, Connecticut to win a formula libre race against the world's greatest sports cars.

When the cars lined up for their ten lap heat race, Tat was up against Rex Easton, Gays Biro, Shorty Templeman, and Buddy Cagle.

In the heavy clay of the track, the drivers would throw the car sideways while still on the straightaways and put the throttle to the floor, powering thru the turn sideways in a beautiful arc.

The Pavese car with the two speed rear end did not bog down in the heavy clay as the Offys did. With plenty of power for the corners, Tat, who started on the back row, threw the car into the first turn and walked away from all but one of the nation's best midget drivers.

Johnny Shipman tells how Tat nailed the last one in turns three and four:

"Coming off the fourth turn Tat flipped off his goggles as if to say, Sayonara." At the finish of the five miles, Tat was a half-a-lap ahead of the second place car. When he pulled into the pits he was met by every AAA Official on the grounds.

"You guys are going to have to tear the engine down. You've got to be running oversize."

Tat and Frank just laughed. "Shucks, we're not going to do that. We just came down to show you how a real race car runs."

Pavese took the car to the Terre Haute Fast Track that night and Tat cleaned house, winning everything.

Insiders got a kick out of the episode because everyone knew that Frank Pavese ran a small engine so he could wind it tighter.

It's not nice to fool the big boys.

Now all of midget racing knew what it meant when someone said, "Tattersall's coming."

***

On the west side of Alexandria, Indiana, stood a beautiful banked paved speedway. Like the Sun Valley Speedway in Anderson, Alexandria was one of the fastest tracks on the Car Owners Racing Association schedule.

Because of its location, the track drew cars and drivers from Chicago and Joliet to the west, and Toledo and Grand Rapids to the east.

Some of the name drivers at that time were Charlie Mayer, known as "The Preacher," "Gentleman" Bob Reemsnyder, Tommy Gray "The Silver Fox," and Eddie "Bootie" Yeager.

Bud Bogard and Gene Rodgers were the top CORA drivers at the time and for a bunch of outlaws, the feature race at Alexandria was of excellent quality.

In 1957 I was making the transition from the grand-stands to the track. I was in awe listening to the stories and just being around race drivers. After having watched these drivers race for a couple of years, I was aware that these were not just a bunch of weekend racers.[2]

Working the pit gate at a race track is a fun experience. By the time the gate opens there is usually a large crowd ready to sign in and receive their credentials.

It is during this time that the fellowship, joking and needling takes place. Once inside there is work to do.

Such was the scene this night at Alexandria. We were about to open the pit gate and some twenty teams were already lined up to sign in.

"Tattersall's coming!"

One minute everyone was cutting up and the next, a wildfire broke loose.

I had seen Bob Tattersall win the heat race at Terre Haute and knew he was one tough race driver, but so were these guys.

There must have been twenty conversations going on at once, all expressing fear.

"Tattersall's coming!"

That's all it took. Two words and total chaos.

There couldn't have been a stronger reaction if some-one had said Jesus was coming.

In ten minutes the entire bunch had psyched them-selves out of first place, and if Willie came with Tat, second place was gone also.

As it turned out Tattersall and Willie stayed home that night. By feature time, the racers were so strung out that it was one of the most competitive races CORA ever ran.

Tat and Willie did show up on July 7th. Tat was third quick, won the dash, was second in his heat and won the feature.

[2]Ed Watson.

The dynamic duo also raced at the Indianapolis Speedrome a year later. Bud Bogard was winning everything in CORA that year and the pair from Chicago had come to challenge.

Bud Bogard was a working man. He drove heavy equipment for a living. The father of three children, Bud loved to race but it wasn't all he liked to do.

"Those guys like to set people up and then give them a ride," exclaimed Bogard. "They're not going to get a shot at me!"

Sure enough, in the feature Tat got in front of Bud and as soon as Willie drove in behind, Bud headed for the infield.

No one ever made fun of him for leaving the race.

"Those two guys are crazy!" exclaimed Bogard. And everyone knew it.

Bud Bogard won five Car Owners Racing Association Championships. I don't recall him ever wrecking. In 1960 and 1961 he raced several times against Tattersall's Australian companion, Leroy Warriner and won.

Such was the reputation of Bob Tattersall in the late 50's and early 60's.

***

Leo Melcher, a member of the promoting team at the Joliet Stadium, and the man who gave Tat his first sprint car ride, acquired a rather unusual souvenir from Tat.

Leo was the flagman and worked from the inside of the track. At the start of the feature, Tat made one of his famous "drop of the green charges" from the back of the pack to first, picking off Leo in the process. After a double somersault twenty feet into the air, Leo landed with a broken leg.

Tat came up to where Leo was lying on the ground and asked.

"What happened to you?"

After the explanations, Tat informed Leo, "You'll be all right. I'll see you back here next week."

He was![3]

That same year Johnny Riva caught flagman, Mike King up against the fence and took him out. UARA and Joliet was a rough place to race.

***

Wayne Adams was among the major writers who helped shape the legend:

Chicago, IL Feb 25, 1957. We have commented several times in this column about the driving talents of one Bob Tattersall of Streator, Illinois who has been driving midgets and stocks for the past few years and who has been at the top or near the top of the United Auto Racing Association midget ratings for the past couple of seasons. Tattersall who demonstrated to the racing world that he has the talent and that car owner Frank Pavese of Gary, Indiana has the fastest Ford midget in the world swept the NASCAR midget racing series at Daytona Beach in Memorial Stadium. At last report Tattersall had whipped the Offies soundly; has won nine consecutive races, winning three main events and six prelims. I firmly believe this fellow can win any race in the world if his equipment stays together. He's another Tony Bettenhausen.[4]

***

Tat loved riding motorcycles and raced TT cycles as a hobby. Stock car racing offered prize money and cars were safer than the two wheelers. Racing two and three times a week, Tat, with his Granatelli engine, was making news.

After his first midget ride, in the Art Ross car, fans would see him pilot the Dale Pierce #38 and Al Huth's

[3]Eileen Terry: Ed Watson's USAC Midget Yearbook 1972.
[4]Wayne Adams, MidWest Whispers. Illustrated Speedway News.

#88 before Elio Negrelli put him in his car.

The red #13's performance improved under the driving talents of the man from Streator.

Leo Melcher began to comment on Tat's driving style, describing his quick moves on the track as those of a gnat darting about.

"Tat the gnat," somebody said.

The "Tat" stuck.

In the early 50's UARA was a stock block club. No Offies were allowed. In 1954 Tat won a feature at the 87th Street Speedway beating Ken Rubright, Wild Willie, Tony Lenti and Bud Abraham.

In 1955 Tat won four victories in a row at Joliet, a feat that had not been done up to that time.

He placed third in the points that year.

Early in his career he was teamed up with both Jim Hurtubise and Johnny Rutherford. He also raced against a youngster named Parnelli Jones and the old pro, the great Tony Bettenhausen.

Tat would tell writer, Dusty Frazer, "I owe a lot to Tony Bettenhausen. I was pretty cocky at first. I started getting on my head and into wrecks. The car was always bent up until Tony took hold of me and taught me the way to go."[5]

There were rides in the Charlie Ross/Bud Simmons "Reliable Welding" car including the unheard of 500 lap races at the Sun Valley Speedway in Anderson, Indiana.

Elio Negrelli and Frank Pavese were two others who had a lot to do with Tat's success. The owner of the red #13 became the chief mechanic on the Frank Pavese team and suggested Tat as one of the drivers.

By 1955 the Pavese V8/60 s were as famous as their two drivers, Bob Tattersall and Wild Willie Wildhaber.

---

[5]Dustin Frazer, Stock Car Racing Mag.

(Top Left) **Tat with Bob Wilkinson and Bill Finkle at Mazon, Illinois.**
Dee Tattersall Collection.
(Top Right) **Tat and Joe Gersick at Mazon, Illinois.** *Dee Tattersall Collection.*
(Center Left) **Bob with the B-29 in 1951. The door carries the name "Bob" (Lover Boy).** *Dee Tattersall Collection.*
(Center Right) **A happy Frank Ligori carries Bob after a win at the Streator 3rd St. Speedway. Ralph Gallup looks on.** *Dee Tattersall Collection.*
(Below) **Bob Tattersall #59 at the Streator Speedway in 1951.** *K.A. Goodrich photo.*

(Top Left) **Winning in the Stock Cars.** *Ross Photo.*
(Top Right) **Elio Negrelli, Tat and Joe Baris work on the Pavese Ford 60 at Daytona Beach in 1957.** *Dee Tattersall Collection.*
(Left) **Joliet Stadium 1953. Tat in the Al Huth #88. Leo Melcher is the flagman.** *Dee Tattersall Collection.*
(Right) **Tat with the great Tony Bettenhausen.** *Dee Tattersall Collection.*
(Below) **Tat #55 gets taken out by two opponents at Mazon on Aug. 17, 1953.** *Dee Tattersall Collection.*

Tat flipping the Lockard Sprinter at New Breman. Tat told Dee afterwards that he was holding on for all he was worth. Check out his hands.
Dee Tattersall Collection.

(Top) **Frank Pavese and Tat with the famous #27 at Daytona Beach. 1957.**
Dee Tattersall Collection.
(Below) **The famous Pavese Race Team. Tat #27, Frank Pavese, Elio Negrelli,
Willie Wildhaber #67.** *Dee Tattersall Collection.*

Yea, though I walk through the valley of the shadow of death, I will fear no evil; for thou art with me. Psalms 23:4.

8
1957

The Pavese Ford 60 was as unique as its owner. This wasn't just another V8-60. It was a cross-fire Ford 60 which was the product of the Edlebrock Company, a manufacturer of racing heads and manifolds.

The engineering on the motor was a masterpiece. Someone at Edlebrock determined that when a piston on the right bank of the V8 was coming up on the compression stroke, a piston on the left side was coming up on the exhaust stroke.

What would happen if a special cam was made so that both pistons would be coming up on the compression stroke and the two spark plugs were fired at the same time? The result would be like joining two four cylinder engines to the same crank shaft.

There were several crossfire V8-60s around but most sounded like popcorn poppers and did not run all that well.

The Edlebrock engine of Frank Pavese did! It was a factory engine and was maintained by them. When it broke or needed an overhaul, Frank replaced it in the car and sent the bad engine back to California.

When Tat got hooked up with Pavese he was history in the making.

He not only dominated the Joliet Stadium and the Daytona Memorial Stadium, he dominated every outlaw race he showed up for.

Soon he was being called the "King of the Outlaws."

In 1956 Tat won the UARA Championship.

When the Pavese team headed for Florida the following February Tat also had a sprint car ride with Leo Melcher for the IMCA races.

1957 was to be a big year!

The season started with the sprint cars at Tampa. In five races, Tat had placed tenth in two features, won a heat and scored two seconds and one third in the other heats while driving Leo's 265 Chevy against the more powerful Offenhausers.

The four days of midget racing at Daytona was much more productive. Tat scored three clean sweeps before the car broke on the fourth day.

Nevertheless, he made track history with nine wins in a row.

The United States Auto Club which had taken over when AAA quit the sport of auto racing in 1956, opened its outdoor season with a Tangerine Tournament for midget cars. In the eleven race series, Tat won two heats against the Offys and managed to make two features, placing 3rd in one.

It was during the IMCA days that Tat and Bobby Grim became life long friends.

Tat made several new friends out there when the Florida season was over. One of them was Russ Moyer — the promoter of the Reading Fairgrounds. The famous promoter saw all the press coverage one Bob Tattersall was getting and began work to assure that this crowd pleaser got to his race track.

Jud Larson had charged out of the Oklahoma sprint cars into the USAC spotlight in the rich Hoosier Hundred Championship race. His USAC sprint car ride was the famous Pfrommer Offenhauser.

Joltin Jud was going to Indianapolis in 1957 and

Moyer suggested that John put the hard-charging Tattersall in his car.

Pfrommer signed the Streator Streak before Sam Traylor could and history was about to be made.

Russ Moyer is sparing no effort to keep his Reading Fairgrounds oval on top in the eastern sprint car racing as he prepares for the Eastern USAC Sprint Car Opener on Sunday, March 31st. The scene of many thrilling duels the Reading opener will unveil a new driving sensation who bids to outshine every other driver who ever appeared in the east. With Jud Larson out of dirt track competition until after the 500 mile classic. Car owner John Pfrommer wasted no time signing up Bob Tattersall of Streator to pilot his blue and white speedster. From reports out of Daytona Beach Tattersall has a style which many say even the daring Wally Campbell would never have attempted. With a cross-fire Ford V8 midget Tattersall ran roughshod over many an Offy in Fla. and all eyes will be on him to see how he can handle the extra Offy power of a sprinter over a half mile track. Tattersall will receive an acid test from the likes of Tommy Hinnershitz, Johnny Thompson, Van Johnson, Eddie Sachs plus an expected western invasion from Elmer George, Don Branson, Len Sutton and Ed Elisian.[6]

Not only was Sam Traylor after Tat, but Dizz Wilson, the speed shop owner from Mitchell, Indiana, hoped to land the Streator sensation for his new sprinter.

Tat's career was about to make a big jump!

***

There are certain points in one's life when opportunities knock. When they do, you have to cut it or else. Tat was ready for the challenge.

Reading proved to be a disappointment for Pfrommer. His car would not run.

George and Francis Littenberger had an Offy sprint car with a small bore engine in it. The car had not done well against the bigger motors.

With the Pfrommer car out, Tat was offered a ride in the Littenberger car. He amazed everyone by qualifying seventh and placing second in his heat race. He placed 12th in the feature after being hit by Jim Packard which bent the front axle.

One week later the USAC Sprints went to Williams Grove. The Pfrommer car proved itself, as did its driver, with second quick time for the day. Ralph Ligouri was the quickest.

The two became friends and when Ralph found out that Dee's maiden name was Ligori he began to tell people they were cousins.

"Dee, how come Ralph spells Ligouri with a "u" and you don't? I thought you were cousins?"

"Hey, if Ralph wants to be my cousin, he can be my cousin."

Sprint car great and Indianapolis veteran, Tommy Hinnershitz, won his heat with the Streator Streak right behind him.

"We're almost there," exclaimed Pfrommer. Let's change that right rear and see if we can't make it better."

It was the wrong move and Tat finished ninth in the main.

Not too bad for a man's first ride in a big Offy!

On the next Sunday, March 14th, the USAC Sprints journeyed to Atlanta, Georgia and the famous Lakewood Speedway. It was a day both Jim Packard and Bob Tattersall would remember. Both flipped in nasty crashes.

The Pfrommer sprinter experienced trouble with the magneto which would not fire. They fooled with the car all through warmups and finally Tommy Hinnershitz loaned them one.

By now it was time to qualify.

Tat asked for a couple of extra laps before getting the green flag as he had not run one single lap on the mile track.

His request was refused.

On the warmup lap Tat was moving. With no knowledge of the track, Tat took the green flag and drove the car deep into turn one. He was really sailing when the car caught a rut and flipped end for end.

It would be his most serious crash!

The doctors were still working on the broken shoulder in Crawford Long Hospital when Elmer George took the checkered flag in the feature that day.

The burns had been cared for and fifty-seven stitches closed the slit throat the windscreen had opened. The broken ribs were taped and the spinal injury would just take time.

"It will be at least six weeks before he will be up and around," the doctor warned.

When the hospital released Tat three days later, Dee took him to her sister's in Mississippi for two more days of rest before making the long trip to Streator.

On March 20th, just six days after the crash, the stitches were removed from Tat's neck. He was still down because of the spinal injury. It was a time when Tat was really scared; not of the injury, but afraid he would have to quit racing. He couldn't walk and when he looked down he would pass out.

Nine days later he called Dee into the bedroom.

"I gotta get up! I'm not going to lay here in this bed."

By the next afternoon he was up.

Nineteen days after the crash he was at the doctor's office in Streator being checked out.

Twenty-three days after the wreck that was to have laid him up for six weeks, Bob Tattersall gingerly lowered himself into Jack Cunningham's USAC midget race car at Oklahoma City and won a heat race. He went on to place third in the USAC feature which was won by Texan Lloyd Ruby.

Three days later he won both the heat and the feature at Wichita, then repeated his first and third place finishes at Kansas City. That race was won by another Texan, A.J. Foyt.

TAT'S BACK! exclaimed the papers.

They were right.

Tat's back needed more rest.

Seventeen days later he took the Tony Saylor #66 to the night before the 500 race. He missed the show with a sick race car.

On June 1st, Tat added another first to his list. He flagged the races at Joliet.

The next day it was off to Toledo, Ohio and another USAC midget race.

Al Willey's midget was ready to race. Tat set a new ten lap record on the half mile track. Running sixth in the main looked good until a car slid in front of him. Tat went up over his wheels and flipped five times, bringing out the red flag.

The neck wound was re-opened, a lung was punctured and he had two broken ribs.

They released him from the hospital three days later.

Four days later he raced the Tony Saylor car at Santa Fe Speedway in Chicago and it was back to the races.

Tat was a terror in the midgets for the next month.

In early July he took Dee and Mickey east with him on a promotional tour for a race in Rochester, New York. Tat left both of them in a motel next to a school yard out in the middle of nowhere while he did his P.R. work. There was nothing to do and without a car, no place to go, they were ready to kill him.

The east coast promoters loved bringing Tat to their tracks and publicized a feud between him and Johnny

Coy who was winning everything in NASCAR Midget competition. They went so far as to print that Johnny Coy would rather beat Bob Tattersall than drive in the Indianapolis 500.

Tat was second quick at Rochester and won a heat, but had trouble in the feature.

A drive through Canada soothed Mickey and Dee's hurt feelings.

On July 14th there was a party at Wildhaber's. Before long Tat and Willie were loaded and playing with the motorcycles.

CRASH!

"Doc, can you sew up my neck?"

Tat continued to win races, set records and even drive a few more sprint cars in 1957. He didn't flip again until August 24th at Joliet when he established the flag pole record.

George Sellery won the UARA Championship.

Tat won eight feature races at Joliet and the Stadium Championship.

One thing about it. People were beginning to recognize the name Bob Tattersall.

Reading Fair

AGRICULTURAL AND HORTICULTURAL
ASSOCIATION OF BERKS COUNTY

READING, PENNSYLVANIA

PENNSYLVANIA'S FINEST AGRICULTURAL FAIR

EXECUTIVE OFFICE
522 COURT STREET
READING 4-8381

March 6, 1957

Bob Tattersall
Auto Race Driver
P.O. Box 276
Streator, Ill.

Dear Bob:

John Pfrommer tells me you will chauffeur his sprint car in our races here
Sunday afternoon, March 31.

Was mighty glad he landed you, because I told him of your exploits in the
NASCAR midgets at Daytona Beach.

Have only one observation: If you chauffeur his sprinter like you did the
midget, you're a cinch to stand the fans on their heads at Reading.

At your earliest convenience, will you kindly send me a recent 8 by 10 closeup
head shot of yourself for publicity purposes. Send it to the address at the
top of this letter.

Also give me you home phone number for my files.

Again, welcome to the east, particularly Reading.

Respectfully,

Russ Moyer
Race Director

(Top) **Russ Moyer letter.**
(Below) **The famous Pfrommer Sprinter at Reading, Pa. in 1957. L to R.
Bummer Ellis, John Pfrommer, Sr., John Pfrommer, Jr.** *Walter T. Chernokal photo.*

WILSON MOTORS
INDIAN MOTORCYCLES AND SPEED EQUIPMENT
MITCHELL, INDIANA

Mar 7 – 1957

Dear Bob:

Saw where you were doing all right in the Midgets in Fla. as long as it stayed glued together and was wondering if you were about ready to drive an Offy big car.

(I'm building a new one (almost completed) and will have an Offing in the 70 or 71 big race time. Guess we run Newport Tenn. some time in early April. Think you would do all right in an Offy and if you're available want you to contact me soon as I want to possibly split the team between national speedways and auto Racing when they are both racing on the same day.

I've had my phone removed temporary but you can call me through the Ford store Ge next door - phone R - or Write? Think we would have a pretty good 1-2-3 punch if we get organized esp at St paul as that is our biggest dates - be seein you

Sincerely

E. M. "Dizz" Wilson

(*Top*) Dizz Wilson letter.
(*Below*) Bob and Dee after his wreck in the Pfrommer Sprinter.
Dee Tattersall Collection.

Iron sharpeneth iron; so a man sharpeneth the countenance of his friend. Proverbs 27:17.

9
1958

With Dee and Tat's seventh wedding anniversary approaching, Tat decided to throw a huge party.

"Tat, we don't have any room to throw a party. You can't get ten people in this trailer, and you sure as the devil can't have a party outside on the 13th of November!"

"Aw, Dee, you got no spunk. We'll clear out the tire shed and clean it up. It'll be a great place for a party."

Letters were sent out, phone calls made, and the party was on.

No sooner than Tat, Dee and her mom had started cleaning up the tire room, Tat came down with strep throat.

Dee and her mom continued the job of moving all the heavy tires and cleaning the room while Tat went to the doctor who decided to tie off the highly inflamed uvula.

"It'll shrink and just drop off," the doctor told him. Sure enough, Tat was well the day of the party.

The following day Mom would be in the hospital with a bad back.

It was a great party! Dee's special present to Tat still remains as a show piece in the living room; a giant scrapbook, with a wooden back and cover. It features three race cars with a checkered flag and the words "My BOB" on the front. The scrapbook already contained clippings from the 1957 season.

*****

Sprint car racing had not been good to Bob Tattersall, but it had given him a great deal of attention.

The press picked up on his quick recoveries from injuries and his ability to come charging back.

Tat was now piloting the Saylor Offy and the races at Daytona's Memorial Stadium made him a tiger the rest of the year. Willie Wildhaber was in the Pavese Ford 60 Tat had done so well with the previous season and Willie beat Tat in two of the four races. "Shucks, anyone can win with this car," chided Willie.

Tat was furious. He hated getting beat, especially by a friend.

The NASCAR series continued on the east coast and Tat decided to go for both the NASCAR and UARA titles, which didn't leave much time for trucking with an eighty race schedule.

Right after New Years another card came from Willie. It said, "Happy New Year." Then in parenthesis with an arrow pointing to the greetings was, "Bull." Signed, Willie.

Tat agreed. A new year of trucking would be bull. 1958 would be all race cars.

Unknown to Bob Tattersall, other people were being made aware of his presence. One such man was Kym Bonython from Adelaide, South Australia.

The people from "Down Under" were no strangers to midget race cars. They had imported the magnificent machines to their tracks in 1938, just five years after they first appeared at Ascot Speedway in Los Angeles, California.

The Australians history of midget racing is as rich and wonderful as that of the United States and the Australian promoter from Adelaide was as big a story as the American driver he was about to import to his lovely country.

Bonython had been a RAAF pilot during the war. He raced cars and speed boats, had a submarine, owned an art gallery and was very involved in all aspects of the music business. From his handwriting he should have been a brain surgeon.

He and Tat shared like interests, however, as his book title *"Ladies' Legs and Lemonade"* tells, he never acquired the taste for liquor. Bonython had better ways to lose his money. Still, he was right at home in the wild world of auto racing and became a true friend to Bob Tattersall.

Asked as a child to name the three greatest men ever known, Kym Bonython answered, "Major" Henry Seagrave, who broke the land speed record when Kym was seven, Jesus Christ, and Dr. Gunson," the family physician.

Dirt track "Speedway" racing began in Adelaide, in 1926 while Kym was a lad.

In 1949 he watched youthful Jack Brabham race at Kilburn Speedway. Brabham went on to win three Formula One Championships and received Knighthood. He also started the rear engine revolution at Indianapolis.

In 1954 Kym leased a soccer stadium which had been built on the site of an old clay quarry and could not support grass due to the saline earth. It was called "Rowley Park."

Rowley Park held races on Friday night enabling the drivers to run Melbourne or Sydney on Saturday. Brisbane, which was 1500 miles away, also ran on Saturday.

Australian racing differed from American by running what Americans called a split show.

The Australians raced motorcycles, with and without sidecars, several kinds of stock cars, and midgets, known to the Australians as "speedcars."

This type of show was a huge success and was copied by the Americans when U.S. promoters heard about the crowds "Down Under."

Running the many different types of races on one night brought fans to the track by the thousands. It was nothing to see 10,000 to 20,000 people watching an event.

During a trip to the United States, Kym met a fast-talking, voluptuous Italian girl, Bobbie Borghese, at Duke Donaldson's Freeport Track on Long Island. Bobbie was one of the first foreigners to race at Rowley Park and did well in the Powder Puff Derbies.

The idea for Demolition Derbies was also imported and became a huge success with the fans.

There were also trips to England, Sweden and Denmark looking for talent among the bike riders.

New England's Dick Brown was Kym's first United States speedcar import. Brown's success had the Adelaide promoter looking for other top foreign drivers.

Joe Barzda was a very good sprint, midget and championship dirt car driver who owned a speed shop on the east coast. He was a big supplier of speed parts and cars to Australia, and Bonython was one of his biggest customers. It was Barzda who recommended that Kym take the sensational Bob Tattersall "Down Under."

So, in the summer of 1958 an offer to go to Australia for the winter season of 1958-1959 arrived in Streator, Illinois. A fantastic V8/60 would be provided. All expenses would be paid and for fourteen races, Bob would come home with a good winter's wages.

When the hometown fans heard the news they were more excited than Tat was, and Tat developed some real fans in Joliet.

One such follower was John Mooney, an alcoholic who would come to Joliet and always bring a bottle of scotch for Tat. When Tat won, John would come to the pits after the race and give Tat the bottle. Tat would take a big drink and give the bottle back to John to take home with him.

One time John called Mom Ligori's (Tat and Dee did not have a phone at the time) and asked for Tattersall.

"Tat don't live here," Mom told him.

"Well, wipe your rear with mustard," replied John.

John made several of those kinds of calls and the phone company decided to disconnect his service. When the lineman got up on the pole, John set his dogs loose. The police had to come and rescue the Illinois Bell employee.

As popular as Tat was in America, he could not have imagined how popular he would become in Australia. As he prepared to leave for his first winter tour, the promoters at the Chicago Amphitheater held a "Bob Tattersall Send Off Nite" indoor race. Bob won the race and led the indoor points over Buddy Martin, Johnny Roberts, Landy Scott, Ernie Sarder, Pete Peterson and Bud Williams.

Kym Bonython was at the airport to welcome the American ace who would become his greatest import.

Bob Tattersall had come to add his name to those American drivers who had won the Australian Championship. Names such as Paul Swedberg, Cal Niday, Frank "Satan" Brewer, and Dick Brown.

Others went down several times but Tat was invited again and again for 13 years.

Bob and Dee made such an impression on the country that in 1977 when Sydney's Channel 7 did the show "This Is Your Life Kym Bonython," Dee was flown down to be on the program.

Among the imports who tasted Australian dirt were several National Midget Champions including, 1953 AAA Midget Champion, Leroy Warriner; the 1952

Champ Johnnie Tolan; 1963's Bob Wente; and 65 and 66 charger "Iron" Mike McGreevy.

Mel Kenyon, who at the time of Tat's death, was a three time USAC Champion and had won six more USAC races than Tat, also went Down Under.

The list includes the 1978 Indianapolis Co-Rookie of the Year, Larry Rice, who traveled Down Under for several years after Tat died.

Marshall Sargent, Jimmy Maguire, Sherman Cleveland, Hank Butcher, Jimmy Kirk, Don Meacham, Billy Mehner, Merle Bettenhausen, Dave Strickland, Stan Fox, John Hubbard, Len Duncan and Sleepy Tripp also saw action in Australia, not to mention Johnny Rutherford and A.J. Foyt. However, none could come close to Tat's popularity or record.

Jimmy Davies, driver of Pat Clancey's six wheeler at Indianapolis and three time National Midget Champion, went Down Under for the 1963-64 season. Davies won fifty-three of fifty four races but was not liked by the Australian fans or competitors because of his arrogant and outspoken attitude.

Kym's first ride in an Offy was in the Davies car which Les Scott purchased after Jim was killed in it at Santa Fe Speedway in Chicago in 1966. Scott brought the car back to Australia in 1972.

"Jimmy Davies was one of the most accomplished race drivers to ever appear on the speedways of Australia, but as good as he was, he met his match in the incomparable Bob Tattersall, who was without doubt the best driver I ever imported," said Bonython in his book, "*Ladies' Legs and Lemonade*."[7]

[7]*Ladies' Legs and Lemonade,* Index:
ISBN 0 7270 1191 x, By: Kym
Bonython, published 1979 by
Rigby Limited.

(Top) L to R. Hedley McGee, Mike Raymond, Dee Tattersall, Kym Bonython, Joan and Howard Powers. *Dee Tattersall Collection.*
(Left) Dee and Kym Bonython. *Dee Tattersall Collection.*
(Lower Left) Tat doing a TV promotion. *Doug Balmer photo.*
(Lower Right) Publicity photo released by Deke Houlgate-Public Relations.
Caption: Farewell Kisses — USAC Midget star Bob Tattersall of Streator, Ill., gets a warm sendoff from his wife, Delores, left, and trophy girl Sue Reilly, who saw him off when he boarded P&O Line's Oriana at Port of Los Angeles.

Jimmy Davies and Tat. *Dee Tattersall Collection.*

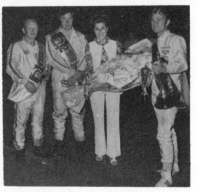

Dee presents Dave Strickland the Bob Tattersall Memorial Trophy in 1972 at Auckland NZ. Barry Pinchbeck and Ron Mackay look on. *Bruce Kent photo.*

Dave Strickland gets a kiss from Dee.

(Above) John Mooney. World Derby winner 1967. *Ian Smith*

Man goeth forth unto his work and to his labor until the evening. Psalms 104:23.

10
Australia

Australia and America share much in common, both in size and culture. If we took the United States and bent it into a downward arc, redrew the Texas shore line from its western boundary in a gentle upward curve to Dallas and then down to New Orleans, turned Florida sideways and shoved it up against Mississippi, Alabama and Georgia, and pushed the upper Northeastern states over until Maine touched upper Michigan, we would have the continent of Australia.

From the Mississippi River to the West Coast would be desert and the eastern mountains would be where the Mississippi River is.

New Orleans would be called Adelaide; Tallahassee would be named Melbourne; Sydney would be on the South Carolina coast; New York would be called Brisbane; and Ascot Park would be located in Perth, not Los Angeles.

For the Australian reader, Joliet Stadium would be around Clancurry. Winton would be the home of the 500, The Oklahoma and Kansas races would be in the area of Alice Springs. Daytona Memorial Stadium would be at Bass Strait and Reading and Williams Grove would be a little west of Rockhampton.

In the late 50's you could drive most anywhere in the U.S. on two lane black top roads.

In Australia you could go by train, plane, boat or drive dusty dirt roads.

When the Americans had had enough of England's King they went to war. With no place to dump unwanteds, the King sent them to Australia.

Both countries were settled by people who had to tear a living from the earth. People who worked hard, played hard, and loved a good time.

Australia was rich in ore from the earth and became a mining country along with livestock.

America became an industrial country.

Australia an importer of industrial goods.

Miners and factory workers shared long hours, hard work, and boredom. Auto racing helped cure the latter.

Auto racing flourished in Australia at the same time it did in America. After the second World War the sport hit its highest peak.

Because the Australians promoted so many different types of racing on a single night's program, midget racing did not get a chance to shoot itself in the foot from over exposure and interfighting as it did in America.

Just as the U.S. had its midget cities such as Los Angeles (Ascot Park), Joliet, Illinois, Sun Prairie, Wisconsin and several cities on the east coast, the Australians had fans in Adelaide (Rowley Park), Melbourne (Traceys), Sydney (The Royale), Brisbane (Exhibition) and Perth (Claremont).

The winter of 1958-59 would see Bob Tattersall racing only at Adelaide. Before the series was over, other promoters would want the American at their tracks.

Bonython was a promoter. Knowing how Tat liked to dress in cowboy clothing, he promptly named him "Two Gun Bob Tattersall." The press had a field day with the name and produced a cartoon with Indians in several cars and the "Cowboy" ready to do battle.

Bonython had purchased a Championship V8-60

midget from New Zealand Champion, Ross Goonan, who would ironically die from cancer.

A full week of press coverage for the first night in the car produced a huge crowd at Rowley Park to see the American cowboy.

Tat was spectacular until the steering broke and he crashed the fence. His first night of racing was spent in the Royal Adelaide Hospital.

The next day, when he was released, the press wanted to know if he would be able to race again.

"I'm awful sore and beat up, but I'll be there Friday night. I've crashed before and come back to win."

And come back he did by winning six of sixteen races and placing no worse than third nine times. He came home with the South Australian Title and was second to Harry Neale in the Australian Championship.

Before Tat headed for home, the agreement had been made for him to return. Empire Speedways which promoted two tracks wanted in on the deal. Tat promised to bring an Offy powered midget with him on the return trip.

There was only one change in the contract.

All expenses would be paid..........EXCEPT TAT'S LIQUOR BILL.

The racers loved Tat because he helped them with their cars. His friendly attitude and great laugh made him a big hit.

The fans loved him because after the race he would sit and drink beer or scotch with them until the lights went out.

An article on Tat that appeared in "Australian Speedway Magazine" tells of the famous "wet your pants episode."

After a Rowley Park meeting Bob and several others were going to a party and Tat was offered a lift with a few of the locals going along. The driver of the car concerned was a youngster and he decided to impress the visiting ace with a display of his own skill around the Adelaide streets.

It takes a lot to raise Tattersall's hair but he hasn't a liking for anyone doing "big things" who doesn't exactly know what he's doing.

In the end it was too much. He calmly moved his foot across, tramped the accelerator to the boards...and held it there, leaving the young Fangio desperately trying to keep the car on the road and steer through traffic.

Naturally enough he went to water.

When Tattersall teaches, he teaches hard.[8]

[8]Australian Speedway-67.

For advertising and correspondence queries address all letters to publishers, Colorado Press, 2 Gilbert Road, Preston, Victoria.

Vol. 3, Issue 2   MELBOURNE, FRIDAY, DECEMBER 12, 1958   Price 6d.

Steering fails: Crowd sees
YANKEE FLIER IN CRASH

ADELAIDE, Dec. 5: Stateside "car-cowboy" Bob Tattersall crashed head-on into the safety fence at Rowley Park Speedway tonite after a sensational steering failure incident.

In the 15-lap feature race his steering packed up and he failed to make a bend. He went straight in and whacked the safety fence a beauty.

His terrifically prepared V8 60 bounced back many feet after the impact. The front end of the car was just a tangled, squashed mess.

Tattersall was assisted from the wrecked car, but tried to re-assure ambulance men he was okay. The tough American limped about for a while, then agreed to go to hospital to have his knee X-rayed.

Tattersall spent the night in Royal Adelaide Hospital and was discharged the following morning. A few minutes after his discharge, he told Speedway Star's Adelaide correspondent, Peter O'Halloran, that no bones had been broken in his knee, and that he thought he would be fit again to race tonight (Dec. 12).

Tattersall said a knock received during the 15-lapper broke the car's exhaust pipe. Heat from the motor was deflected on to the car's steering box. Lubricant in the box dried up and seized the steering.

Tattersall's driving displays proved that he is the most aggressive driver we've seen here for a while. If he gets a clip or a bump he just keeps going, no buttoning off with this rooster. However, he's not unnecessarily reckless.

In the 15-lap feature Tattersall drew position 10 — rear of the field. The leading drivers drew well. Tattersall had trouble forcing a passage through the slow cars. One driver in particular, repeatedly (continued on Page 2)

TQ's AND STOCKS THRILL ADELAIDE CROWD

ADELAIDE, Dec. 5: The TQ's (Flying Fleas) went hammer and tongs at Rowley Park and there was excitement in the four-lap scratch race won by Bert Miller.

Ray Foot, coming fast around a bend had to swing wide to avoid Laurie Jamieson, Alf Bichard and one or two others when they tangled. Foot woodpecked the fence several times and was lucky to be mobile when he stopped against the fence. The ironmongery also flew in the 15-lap stock car marathon.

After a few laps there were cars out of action everywhere. If they weren't upside down they were jammed against the fence. It was a real thriller and only seven remained on their wheels to see out the finish. Winner was Don Furniss from Brian Holness. Clem Smith —who had an early tangle — had a lively tussle throughout with Holness and Furniss. He never kept them out of his sight, although he was a lap behind.

GERMAN RIDER FOR PARRAMATTA

BOARD, McKINLAY CLASH IN MELB. CINDER DUELS

MARIBYRNONG, Dec. 7: "Dasher" McKinlay, John Board and Peter Vandenburg were the solo stars at last week's Melbourne bunfight. Johnny Board rode well on the night and took some tossing when he wound it up and kept it there. ......

Cliff Wallis nabbed the 2nd heat of the solo hep. when he bolted home in front of Peter Vandenburg, with McKinlay a (continued on Page 2)

Parramatta crowds are now to see their latest addition to solo ranks in Grimm Armin, German solo champ of '49-'50 seasons.

Armin was captain of his team during the World Championship and has an impressive Continental record.

A colorful rider with plenty of track "know-how," Armin will be a very worthy asset against the solo boys at the Parramatta track and should adapt himself quickly to this tricky little cinder circuit, that makes bike events so spectacular.

Scottish champ Ken McKinlay has been appearing at Rowley Park, Adelaide, recently. That's him nearest camera. McKinlay is racing in Toowoomba on Dec. 19 and Brisbane on Dec. 20 and 27. After that he's racing in Sydney.

The Star . . . Australia's leading Speedway paper

(Top) Speedway Star headlines first race crash in Australia.
(Below) Tat's first night in Australia at Rowley Park on December 5, 1958 when the steering broke. *Dee Tattersall Collection.*

RIGBY on the Speedway

"Can't let the heap big paleface have it ALL his own way."

Thou wilt show me the path of life. Psalms 16:11

11
1959

Bob Tattersall came home from Australia excited. Running one race a week and winning addicted him to victory lane.

Teamed with Tony Saylor in the Offy he planned to take on the return trip Down Under, Tat also had Leo Melcher's Chevy for the IMCA circuit.

The USAC Sprint cars had bitten Tat hard, and while he never excelled in the powerful machines, he did have some success.

During a three year run with IMCA on a limited basis, Tat broke Frank Luptow's record for a race the Americans called, of all things, "The Australian Pursuit." The object of the race was to pass all the cars without being passed. Each time a car was passed he was out of the race.

The day Tat won the "Pursuit," the last car to go down was driven by Bobby Grim.

During an afternoon race in St. Paul, Minnesota, Tat had fast time and placed third in the feature in spite of losing the brakes during the event. Frank Winkley, who ran IMCA asked Tat and Leo to stay and run more races, offering them $1000 up front.

"I've got to get back to the stadium and win the Championship," was Tat's response.

"Tat, you could stay away for two months and win the Championship," argued Leo.

Tattersall returned to Joliet and the $100 a night paid when he won.

Leo and Tat did go back to Minnesota and won a feature. That day Winkley paid him $200 for the win.

"I didn't invite you and that's what it pays."

So much for IMCA.

Bob also found time to take on the USAC midget gang on eight occasions in 1959 and saw the top ten twice with one second and one sixth place finish; but nothing was going to stop him from going back to Australia without a Championship.

Bob drove Joliet Stadium much smoother now; more relaxed. Winning every night at Rowley Park had taught him just how good he really was.

Late in the season at Joliet after the races, while sitting on the can in the john under the main grandstand, Willie came in and they began to joke about some of the wild races.

"Remember the night you flipped into the maintenance building and Leo welded your broken axle?" asked Willie. "You were sitting where you are right now asking me who won. I told you I did and you ran second. Remember what you said? You said that you had just gotten back from the hospital. You couldn't have run second. Boy were you goofy that nite!"

"Yeah, I was," Tat replied, "But I whipped your tail more than you've whipped mine!"

"Remember the night Pavese offered me the Offy for that 100 lap Feature and I took the Ford instead, and won?"

The two men joked and cut up for a long time. It was as if both knew that their days of racing together were about over.

Tat was well on his way to another UARA Championship and Australia lay at his feet. Deep inside, both men knew that Bob Tattersall was about to move up in the sport of auto racing.

Willie Wildhaber would remain a truck driver who raced cars. His UARA Championship was as high as he'd climb.

There was never any jealousy. Tat had married his girl, beat him as a teammate and succeeded in the same endeavors Willie had tried for. Willie couldn't be jealous, he loved this friend from Streator.

This year the writers were talking about Tat's "wins," not his crashes.

Veteran Bob Tattersall will be out to clinch the 1959 track Championship as midget auto racing enters the home stretch Saturday nite at Joliet Memorial Stadium. Tattersall of Streator has five feature victories to his credit. Three of them in this seasons three 50 lap events. A sixth main event triumph should put Tattersall up ahead of the field to coast home to his second straight track championship and third in four years.

Last weekend's fifty lap victory ended a four week dry spell for Tat, who won his last feature July 4th.

Close competitor in feature victories is Danny Kladis from Chicago who has won two. Bernie Wilhelm of Joliet who placed second to the Streator ace last season has managed only one feature triumph this year. Among the other drivers out for victory Saturday night will be Willie Wilson, Tony Lenti, Bob Tomlinson, Newt White, Aaron Willis and Bob Hauck.[9]

A few weeks later the headlines read:

TATTERSALL WINS CROWN
PREPARES FOR AUSTRALIA

What a way to celebrate an anniversary! A boat trip to Australia!

Dee and Tat had a great cruise, enjoying the lovely days on the blue Pacific with the Saylor Offy stored in the hold of the ship.

They had never had a real honeymoon and in Australia they would be sharing a cottage with the family of English bike rider, Peter Craven.

1959 had been a great year; The South Australian Championship, second in the run for the Australian crown and another UARA Championship.

Bob Tattersall was ready for 1960!

***

The setting was wonderful; a cottage on the seafront at Tennyson not far from Kym Bonython's home. Sharing the cottage was easier than Dee imagined because Peter and Bob were gone on publicity tours most of the time.

Peter's wife, Brenda and their son were good company; however, Dee got homesick before the tour was half over. She remembered the motel in New York; Tat was out running while she stayed behind.

"Guess he'll never change!"

Peter Craven was rather shy and retiring and presented a great contrast to Bob Tattersall with his loud, rough and aggressive personality.

This trip Tat was racing at several tracks, not just Rowley Park. Now it was SHOW TIME in Sydney.

The scene was the Showground Speedway Royale. The sidecar and solo riders had performed before the packed grandstand of 30,000 fans. Australian announcer and writer Allan Edworthy tells it best.

The huge crowd murmurs excitedly and inches forward in anticipation as a gleaming yellow midget speedcar is pushed out onto the track. In stark contrast to the bold '55' emblazoned on the tail, the lettering on the bonnet of the car simply states "Saylor's Offy, USA...Driver Bob Tattersall."

A push-car is guided onto the rear of the racer

and slowly, locked together, the two vehicles move as one. Only yards into the journey the driver releases the hand brake and ignition button simultaneously. Instantly, the oil pressure rises and the powerful Offenhauser engine explodes into life. The unique, throaty sound of the magnificent Meyer and Drake powerplant reverberates through the concrete canyons of the equally magnificent Showground arena.

As the pit gates are slammed shut, scores of drivers, riders and pit crews jostle for positions along the pit wall. The yellow midget is the only car on the track, its shiny paintwork and chrome sparkling beneath the overhead track lights.

Idling around the narrow one-third mile dirt oval, the driver settles into the cockpit and awaits a signal from the officials. Two laps go by and the crowd again edges forward, anxious to get a glimpse of what most know to be a unique ritual. Finally, the green flag is shown and the solitary race car accelerates away.

The sleek midget powers into the first turn, the rear push-bar only inches from the safety fence. The crowd looks on in stunned silence as the car seemingly sits poised on the brink of disaster. But as though connected to some invisible guide-wire, the machine completes a perfect arc to race along the back straight, only to repeat the performance in the next turn. The driver never flinches. He sits perfectly erect, head tilted slightly back and arms pumping like pistons in smooth, decisive movements.

Speeding around the narrow ribbon of dirt, the gutsy four cylinder Offy barks out its war cry as its master sits unperturbed, controlling every movement with such skill and agility that the whole operation seems akin to some majestic orchestration.

The onlookers are held spellbound. Several more laps are completed in this manner before the driver slows and brings the racer to a halt on the main straight. An eerie silence falls over the arena as the driver shuts down the pulsating car and removes his helmet.

The capacity crowd erupts as the announcer shouts into his microphone..."Ladies and Gentlemen...From Streator, Illinois...Bob Tattersall."[10]

The Australians had just witnessed their first "true" power slide. Australian speedcar racing would not be the same again, and neither would Bob Tattersall.

The Royale was the Indianapolis of Australian auto racing. The track hosted the World Midget Speedcar Championship which dated back to 1938. Four Americans had won the event; Paul Swedberg in 1938 and 40, Cal Niday in 1947, Frank Brewer in 1950 and Dick Brown in 1957, for a total of five victories.

Bob Tattersall would win it seven times in eleven tries.

The Royale would become his track!

Rowley Park in Adelaide already belonged to Tat, and while "buzzing the Royale" had everyone talking, Rowley Park was the site of Bob Tattersall's most remembered legendary feat, which happened two seasons later.

The story is best told by the man who saw it first hand. Kym Bonython recorded it in his book, *Ladies' Legs and Lemonade.*[11]

Speedway fans will always remember an incident during Bob Tattersall's visit in 1962. Speed cars are designed so that the bulk of the vehicle's weight bears upon the back wheels and the outside front wheel, with only negligible weight on the inside front wheel. When a well-balanced car is at power this wheel hardly touches the track and often rides several inches above it. The purpose of this seemingly strange adjustment is to place the maximum car weight on the driving wheels.

Bob collided with another car during a championship event at Rowley Park and broke his front axle. The inside front wheel flew off the car and for a lesser driver that would have been the end of the event. But, by skillful manipulation of the throttle, Bob completed the remaining twenty-one laps on three wheels by maintaining power and keeping the axle stub up off the track. He was negotiating other speedcars, who certainly did not give him any special consideration because of the accident, and his completion of the course must surely have been one of the most amazing driving exhibitions ever seen.[11]

Editors note: Tat lost the wheel on the 26th lap. Legend had Tat winning this race, however, he ultimately quit the race with just three laps remaining. He had raced for 21 laps minus brakes which departed with the wheel.

[11]*Ladies' Legs and Lemonade*, ISBN 0 7270 1191 x, By: Kym Bonython, published 1979 by Rigby Limited.

(Top) **Another Win at Joliet. L to R. George Peterson, Chuck O'Day, Tony Saylor, Wynns Oil Rep. and Mike King.** *Dee Tattersall Collection.*
(Lower Left) **Championship Form at Sea.** *Dee Tattersall Collection.*
(Lower Right) **Mike McGreevy and Bob Tattersall getting ready to leave for New Zealand and Australia in December 1966.** *Dee Tattersall Collection.*

A little fine tuning.
Dee Tattersall Collection.

Grooving a tire in 1965.

Tat running IMCA in Leo Melcher's #66 at St. Paul, Minnesota.
Al J. Herman photo.

Tat at Mazon in Leo Melcher's #66.
Dee Tattersall Collection.

Tat Down Under.
Kym Bonython Collection.

The Famous Power Slide in the Saylor Offy
Mike Raymond photo.

The famous 3 wheel drive at Rowley Park appeared in Kym Bonython's book *Ladies' Legs and Lemonade* and was shot by ace photographer David Brock. Used with permission. *Ladies' Legs and Lemonade* published by Rigby Limited.

By me kings reign, and princes decree justice.
Proverbs 8:15.

12
King of Down Under

In two seasons Bob Tattersall had become a hero in Australia. Having won the 1960 World Speedcar Championship it was now time to go after the American title.

The United States Auto Club was the elite auto racing sanctioning body in the U.S.A. USAC sanctioned the Indianapolis 500, the Championship Trail for Indy cars, the Sprint, Stock and Midget divisions as well as land speed records.

Racing in USAC midget competition pitted you against the very best in the business. It also required a good race car if you were to be successful.

In essence, USAC midgets were the World Derby every night. Only the very best drivers were able to travel the long schedule of races on the calendar.

The USAC season started with indoor races in January. In March the schedule moved to Phoenix, Arizona and on to California. In late April the Midwest tracks began to run afternoon races. By the end of May the weather allowed the night races to begin.

During the months of June, July and August the midgets would race three and four nights a week. USAC tried to schedule tracks so competitors could race in one area all week, however, this was not always possible and trips of several hundred miles for a single event were common.

There were swings to the east coast for three or four races before an early fall tour that might head for Denver and the Colorado area. Late fall meant Phoenix, Arizona and California.

In the early sixties only a handful of drivers made the complete tour. By the mid-sixties the number had increased to twenty.

The top drivers in each local area would come to challenge the full time drivers.

The men who ran the full circuit became sharp at what they did. The car owners carried a book with them on how the car was set for each track and the changes made each night to improve the machine.

Sizing up a track and being able to compare a new surface to others gave these professional drivers the ability to race at a new track and break the track record the first night.

Hunger was also a factor. The USAC drivers were always hungry. When Jimmy Davies won his first title in 1960 he earned $11,755 in prize money. In 1965 Mike McGreevy raced one less race and only earned $9,837. By 1970 Jimmy Caruthers won $15,754 which was twice what a good factory worker made, but the travel expenses alone would take most of the money.

The big league was just that; only the best were able to come and play, and stay.

When Bob Tattersall came he stayed and what was so unique was the year round schedule he maintained. For eleven years Tat "raced to win" month in and month out with no let up. Many American drivers went to Australia to have fun. Bob Tattersall went to Australia to win. Being "King of Down Under" felt good, and he wasn't about to give it up.

The same "win every night" attitude was necessary to survive in the USAC Midget Division and Bob Tattersall had that attitude.

Because he was racing in Australia, Tat missed the early races and lost valuable points. By the end of his first full season in pursuit of the National Title, Tat was in fifth place.

Jimmy Davies had raced in 55 races. Bob Wente, who became a great friend to Tat, was second after racing in 44 events. Gene Hartley, a veteran of eight Indianapolis races, was third. The fourth place man ran the same number of races Tat did and beat him with six features to Tat's four. Leroy Warriner, the 1953 National Champion was the man and a friend who would join Tat Down Under in the future.

During the season Tat had raced against Parnelli Jones, Shorty Templeman, Len Sutton, A.J. Foyt, Tony Bettenhausen, Don Branson and the best midget chauffeurs in the world.

Tat finished the season winning the Chicago Indoor race on December 17th and finished fifth in the USAC standings.

Full time racing was a way of life. Many drivers had part time jobs in order to go racing. Bobby Grim worked for an oil company which was a winter job and left him time to race during the warm months. The full time racers had a saying, "If your job interferes with your racing, it's time to quit your job."

Because USAC sanctioned the 500 Mile Race, the Indy drivers might show up on any given night. They were sure to come for the special races. The Turkey Day Grand Prix at Ascot Park in Los Angeles was the oldest midget race in the world. The annual Nite Before the 500, the Hut Hundred, The Indoor Championship at Ft. Wayne, Indiana and the races on the mile tracks at Milwaukee, Springfield, DuQuoin, Langhorne and Indianapolis were the prestige races.

The name United States Auto Club was well chosen. It was a club. It was also a family. Membership into the club was easy, you purchased a card and you belonged. Belonging to the family had to be earned. Auto racing claimed several lives a year and the threat of death was always present, even though nobody dwelled on it. Life was precious and too short to take for granted. If you liked someone they knew it. If you didn't like them, they knew it.

It is unique that in a sport that fosters egotism, so much giving is found. Friendships are real and someone in the family who might not be liked would still be helped when in trouble.

In the early sixties the series was officiated with only four officials who were also part of the family. Bob Stroud was the Supervisor, Jim Blunk the Pit Steward, Johnny Roberts the Flagman and Les Kimbrell the Scorer.

Jim Blunk was over seven feet tall and had a dry wit about him. Everyone respected the big man from St. Louis.

Tat had become good friends with Bob Wente and in 1963 Wente was leading the point battle. One night Tat spun and stopped in the middle of the track. Wente was leading the race and his car was loading up. If Wente slowed down, as cars are required to do during a yellow flag, the engine would foul the spark plugs. So Wente was running as fast as he dared on the yellow. The other drivers were running faster trying to close the gap on the leader.

When Tat finally got to the infield he was furious. Seeing a huge bolder, Tat ran over and gathered it into his arms. By now Jim Blunk had run down to the turn.

Here came Tat, holding the rock like a basketball. "I'll slow that Sonofabitch down," he exclaimed as he struggled toward the track.

Standing in his path, Blunk looked Tat right in the eye and said, "You can't do that. He's from St. Louis."

That was all it took.

During a dusty race at Granite City, Illinois, Les Scott started up front and when the green flag dropped, left everyone in a cloud. Tat started on the back row and worked his way into second place through the swirling dust. When the checkered flag fell, Tat drove up to the starting line.

Joe Finley was standing there and asked Tat, "What are you doing?"

"I came to get my trophy! I won this sucker."

"No you didn't," corrected Joe. Les Scott almost overlapped you. You were last. That checkered you saw was for Scott, who was right behind you. You didn't even finish the last lap."

Joe was right, Les was directly behind Tat when he received the checkered flag and Tat thought the flag was for him. Everyone else slowed when the checkered came out and Tat completed his last lap when he came to the line to get what he thought was his trophy.

***

Once Bob Tattersall began his quest for the USAC Midget Championship, he never placed lower than eighth in the National Standings. For the first three seasons he picked up rides wherever he could. In 1963 Paul Baines from Mattoon, Illinois decided to run the entire circuit. He chose Bob Tattersall as his chauffeur knowing they would not be chasing any promoters for the purse. Tat did not get back from Australia till April that year and the pair only won two features. Tat was eighth in the points, then made up for it by taking the car to Australia and a winning season.

Many of the cars Tat took Down Under were sold to the Australians and it became a good business. Baines did not sell his car to the Aussies but he should have.

When the car returned to the States after a second

season in Australia it was stripped of its engine and most of its parts while sitting on the dock.

In 1964 Tat became the "Hot Shoe" for Jack Stroud. The relationship between these two would write midget racing history.

Jack Stroud had been connected with the sport of auto racing since 1936. He raced big cars and motorcycles around the St. Louis area until 1939 when he ventured west and became involved with the midgets of the UMRA (which later became URA).

In 1946, sportsman Dan Topping, took an entourage of American Midgets to England and Jack was selected as one of the drivers.

Topping was married to actress Lana Turner who also made the trip. Producer, Burt Friedlob took his wife, Eleanor Parker and Jim Cross took Patsy Ryan who was Donald O'Connor's sister.

In order to stir up interest, the Americans divided into teams. Frank Armi was captain of the French team, Frank "Satan" Brewer headed up the English and Stroud the American. Al Hendricks and Fletcher Pierce were also involved in the tour.

Stroud quit driving in 1954 but continued as an owner with such drivers as Red Hamilton, Don Branson, Carl Williams, Eddie Johnson, Bill Homeier, Bud Tingelstad, Tommy Copp, Jim McElreath and Sonny Ates.

Jack loved to win as much as Tat did. He had a gruff voice and many a night you would think the owner and his driver were staunch enemies. One day while running a twin 50 on one of the miles, the two went at it.

Tat had not done well in qualifying and finished near the back in the first fifty lapper. Stroud told him he was coasting. "What are you doing, taking a Sunday drive?" needled big Jack.

"You're not standing on it hard enough."

In the second fifty Tat got with it. Each lap he would pass a car or two. On the forty-second mile he pulled beside the leader.

That's when the engine blew!

Limping into the pits Tat jumped from the car which had a big hole in the block where the rod had exited.

"Was that fast enough? Was I standing on it hard enough that time?"

That season they lost five crankshafts in the car and really tore into Stroud's pocket book.

In 1965 and 66 Tat teamed with Bob Nowicke and placed second and fourth in the standings. He would team with Jack Stroud again and the results would be better.

By 1966 the old guard had given way to the new. Jimmy Davies was killed at Santa Fe Speedway in Chicago. Leroy Warriner had turned to promoting the Indianapolis Speedrome. Shorty Templeman and Jim Hemmings were killed in the same crash at Marion, Ohio in 1962. Tat was in the middle of that one. Shorty clipped a gate post on the backstretch with Tat and Hemmings right behind him. Templeman's flipping mount took out eleven cars including Tat's.

Johnnie Tolan had traveled to Australia with Jimmy Davies. He crashed during a race appearance there and broke his back. His last year with USAC was 1965. Tony Bettenhausen died at the Speedway in 1961. Gene Hartley drove in his last 500 in 1962 and only raced occasionally.

Bob Wente, Mel Kenyon, Mike McGreevy, Don Meacham, Les Scott, Bill Vukovich, Jr., Gary Bettenhausen and Bob Tattersall were the big names now.

Mel Kenyon had won the 1964 title and was on his way to a second, when he was badly burned in a Champ Car wreck. His brother, Don continued to run the car with Mike McGreevy as the driver.

The racing family made a giant get well card for Mel. It showed all the cars crashed in a pile and the #1 car on top. The caption read, "Don't worry Mel, you're still on top."

Bob Tattersall was second to "Iron Mike" in the points that year and took McGreevy to Australia with him.

Mel came back minus the fingers and thumb on his left hand and was second to "Iron Mike" in 1966. He won again in 1967 and 1968.

Mel told people that Bob Tattersall was one of his heroes. They were big rivals and enjoyed beating each other on the track. They did not become close friends. Their life styles off the track were diametrically opposed.

Bob and Pat Wente were close friends with Dee and Tat and like the Grims, homes were shared and there were many parties.

Rob Greentree moved to the United States after running second to Bob Tattersall in the World Derby in 1960 and while he had varied success, he was part of the family.

When he moved to Florida and retired from midget racing, the gang threw a big party for him at the famous "Miller's Restaurant" in Colfax, Indiana.

ROB GREENTREE PARTY

Saturday night was party night as friends said goodbye to Rob Greentree the Australian driver who is moving to Florida to begin a new job. On hand were Bob and Dee Tattersall, Mr. and Mrs. Leroy Warriner, Betty Duman, Mrs. Stoffer, USAC official M.A. Todd and his wife, the Bob Higmans, along with Dave Strickland, Pat Vidan and his wife, Mr. and Mrs. Bob Grim along with Susie, Rick Davidson, Larry Rice, the Fred Height's, Betty Greg and Ed and Sue Watson.[12]

[12]Midget News by Ed Watson: USAC **112** News.

Bob loved parties and it became a habit for his fans to throw a birthday party for Tat each year. Of course the fans at Springfield, Joliet, and Santa Fe Park each brought cakes for his birthday and the rest of the racers enjoyed the multi-celebrations.

Terre Haute and the Hut Hundred always had a big bean dinner after the race and DuQuoin had a watermelon party.

Jerry Miller wrote most of one story about an after-the-race gathering in the pits at Oxford, Indiana.

Tat, Bill Renshaw and Mike McGreevy were invited to a piece of chicken and Tat was sharing with Miller how English woman Faye Taylor flipped him out of one track in the early 1950's. Tat also commented on how unsafe it was to have caged midgets racing cars without them.

"You know, what everybody's overlooked is the fact that when a car with a cage flips and comes into the cockpit of somebody without one you're a dead duck."

It was an afternoon of no particular significance, eating fried chicken and listening to Bob Tattersall tell stories about his twenty years of racing.

The five of us went on eating and listening to Bob talk about midget racing that afternoon in the almost deserted infield at Henry's Speedway. The sun was slipping close to the horizon before we tossed our chicken bones down on the ground and moved away to our cars.[13]

At the famous DuQuoin, Illinois, mile in 1969 the promoters had a water ski team performing during the intermissions on the lake in the infield. After the race Bob told the performers that he could do anything they could. Still in his uniform he was out skiing on one ski. California's Bob Rosen and Mase Cook of the Guarantee Fork Lift car also got into the act on the infield water.

[13]Jerry Miller, Pit Pass, Chronicle-Tribune, Marion, Ind.

The drivers' wives for the most part would sit together at the tracks. For the wives sitting in the stands for four or five hours each night is a boring business. One way to pass the time is to record what each husband is doing. Those with kids were kept extra busy trying to keep the little ones out of mischief.

Bob Wente's kids liked to sit with "Aunt Dee" who was very strict. One night Bob Wente Jr. wanted to sit with her.

"OK, you can sit here but you can't be running around. You have to sit here."

Before long Bobby had to go to the bathroom. Next it was off for a coke. When he came back from his third trip and sat down, Dee raised up and sat on his lap. Several minutes went by and a small voice exclaimed, "Aunt Dee, I can't see."

Bobby Grim drove many races for Coxie Bowman. Coxie's wife Willie, was the voice of the racers. For many years people wondered how auto racing writer, Len Milde, got so many stories. Willie was his source and the one who made sure everyone was informed. She also loved to pull gags. One favorite was sending perfumed horse manure to different people with no return address on the package. These mailings were sent from different places in the U.S.

Les Scott had a collection of automobile tail lights and was always looking for exotic hard to get lenses. One day Dee went out in the parts yard and gathered a box of broken pieces, shipping them to Les without a return address. For years Les thought Willie Bowman had sent them.

Tat loved to give advice to people. One night at Knoxville, Iowa, Alex Toth in Joe Finley's Falcon tangled with Ray Elliott who was in Lou Cooper's Falcon. Ray, having won the battle on the track continued in the race. Alex, who was pitted next to Tat was fuming. "I'm going down and punch that guy out!" exclaimed Toth.

"You'd better stay here," advised Tat. I raced against that old man for years. You ain't got no troubles on the track compared to what you'll have in the pits."

When Elliott came in, Alex headed toward his pit. After walking past three cars, he turned and came back.

"That's the smartest thing you'll do all night," Tat exclaimed.

Tat should have kept his mouth shut. Chuck Weyant's car threw up a dirt clod during the feature race and knocked out two of his teeth.

Weyant remained a friend.

The opening of Joe Shaheen's club at the Springfield Speedway. L to R. Veto Coletto, Bill Puterbaugh, Tat, Chuck Weyant and Bob Wente. *Rocky Rhodes photo.*

(Center) George Hopkins and his son Kenney are all smiles having won the feature race at the Terre Haute Action Track in 1961. *Ed Hitze photo.*
(Lower Left) Tat and Leroy Warriner Down Under. *Dee Tattersall Collection.*
(Lower Right) USAC Midget Supervisor, Bob Stroud, presenting Tat with the trophy at Springfield, Illinois. June 20, 1969.
Rocky Rhodes photo.

Aug. 4, 1968. Terre Haute. Tat on the pole #93, Bob Wente #25, Chuck Arnold #73 and Mike McGreevy #2. *Rocky Rhodes photo.*

(Center) **L to R. Joe Shaheen, Bob Stroud and Tat.** *Rocky Rhodes photo.*

(Lower Left) **Marge Hoffman and Tat cutting up.** *Dee Tattersall Collection.*
(Lower Right) **Look guys, No hands.** *Dee Tattersall Collection.*

Paul Baines #3 in 1962. *Roth's studios.*

Howard Linne's #99 DuQuoin, Ill.

Frank Griffo's Fiat. *Dwight Vaccaro photo.*

Ed Pearson's Offy.

#57 Tat poses with the trophies won during the 1959-60 season in Australia.

Steve Hornyak Offy.

Bob Lithgow always gave Tat a ride when he needed it.
Dee Tattersall Collection.

The Howard Linne Race Team. #93 Don Branson, #99 Bob Tattersall, #96 Tony Bettenhausen. *Dee Tattersall Collection.*

USAC Pit Steward, Jim Blunk, with Tat as he prepares to qualify at Davenport, Iowa in the Gus Sohm Offy. *Howard Wiegand photo.*

Ralph Wilkie's Leader Card Offy 1962. *Ed Hitze photo.*

The Goff Offy. San Jose, California 1964. *Gail Alloway photo.*

Bob Nowicke's car at Muncie, Indiana May 26, 1966. *Ed Hitze photo.*

Ed Loniewski Offy. *Rocky Rhodes photo.*

Tat in Howard Linne's car at Milwaukee, Wisconsin in 1960.

Tat at Charleston, Illinois the night he chased the promoter. *Paul Baines*

(Center) L to R. Mickey Ligori, Jack Stroud, Tat, Bob Stroud.
Rocky Rhodes photo.

(Lower Left) Joe Shaheen.
Rocky Rhodes photo.

If thou wilt be a servant unto this people this day, and wilt serve them, and answer them, and speak good words to them, then they will be thy servants forever. I Kings 12:7.

13

Two Gun

When Empire Speedways joined Kym Bonython in promoting Bob Tattersall none of those involved could imagine the tremendous history that would be made during the next eleven years.

At the helm of Empire Speedways were two of the most astute business men Australian Speedway has ever seen, former rider Frank Arthur and John Sherwood.

Both parties hit on the formula that proved a smashing success at the box office. In 1960 Bob Tattersall was introduced to the hotbed of Australian midget racing — the Sydney Showground Speedway.

It was a magnificent arena capable of holding 35,000 fans. The circuit was a one-third mile egg-shaped dirt track. Unlike the wide open spaces of American Speedways, the Showground was very narrow. Tat loved it and dominated it from the first time he rim rode the Showground walls.

Empire Speedways also promoted the Brisbane Exhibition Ground track and while Tat enjoyed success on this tight, saucer-shaped quarter mile, it was the Sydney Showground where he became the Australian Legend.

Arthur and Sherwood picked up the "Two Gun" handle established by Kym Bonython during Tat's first tour and Bob played the part to the hilt.

Tattersall once told the media during a Sydney press

conference, "I had heard so little about Australia when I was offered a contract to come here but I had heard about your kangaroos and your horse racing. I figured that the more colourful I dressed the better impression I would make."

"It was a gimmick, but the outfit helped to put me over well and drew crowds. I was soon taken to heart by Speedway fans, which is good business for me," he added.

John Sherwood related the story of the time he took Tat to lunch at the Royal Automobile Club of Australia in downtown Sydney. Dressed in "cowboy" styled clothes, it did not take long for Tat to become the centre of attention in the RACA dining room, as he preached the virtues of midget auto racing to his captive audience.

The western style clothes gradually disappeared, but those early years as the "cowboy" helped make the legend.

With the success of the first couple of tours, Tattersall was asked to select a touring partner for his Down Under jaunts. Leroy Warriner, the 1953 AAA National Champion was the first to go for the 1961-1962 season.

The soft-spoken Warriner was impressed and returned for a second season. Tattersall's 1961 car was an older Kurtis-Kraft that had done many miles. The following year he had the sleek Cascio Offy. Leroy brought cars that were sleek and fast and both were purchased by Don Mackay, a leading Sydney car owner.

Leroy Warriner was involved in a race that still has the local Adelaide fans talking.

The date was February 2, 1962, and Bob Tattersall stole the show with his three wheel balancing act at Rowley Park during the Australian Speedcar Derby. The amazing run by Tat overshadowed a great race between Warriner and local driver, Ron Wood. Warriner had come from the back of the field and placed a close second to Wood at the finish. He was closely pursued by Victorian, Billy Humphries, who later enjoyed success racing in America.

Although Tat ultimately quit the race with three laps remaining, the supershow is still the most talked about feat in Australian racing history.

In 1963 the legendary three time USAC National Midget Champion, Jimmy Davies, accompanied Tat to Australia.

For his first visit he brought his own famous Offy with him. A smooth, calculated driver, Davies won more than his share of major races on that tour. Meanwhile, Tattersall was aboard the beautiful Mattoon Motors black #3 Offy.

Many Australians believe this was the best car Bob ever brought to Australia. The advance publicity on the car centered around the reasoning behind why Tat chose the car for his Australian commitments.

As the story goes, the car was owned by a Miss Julia Simms who, after watching Tat race at Ascot Park in California, asked Bob to take it to Australia. Bob accepted the offer from Miss Simms, whose backing was the Mattoon Motors Chrysler Corporation in Illinois.

A woman car owner and a major corporation was great hype, however, the true story finds Tat's old friend, Paul Baines owning the car while Miss Simms was the car's sponsor. She owned Mattoon Imperial Motors, which was a Chrysler dealership in Mattoon, Illinois.

The sleek racer ran as well as it looked. The first night out in Australia at the Sydney Showground on December 22, 1963, Bob Tattersall took out the entire speedcar programme, and in winning the feature race from Jeff Freeman and Johnny Peers, took 9.2 seconds off the track record for the 25 lap distance.

Jimmy Davies also captured plenty of headlines and

enjoyed tremendous success in Australia. Davies had traveled to Indianapolis seeking information on Australia racing from Leroy Warriner. Leroy asked Davies how many gear changes he planned to take with him. Davies told him he'd only planned to take a couple. "There isn't much competition down there," he remarked.

"What about Tattersall?" asked Leroy.

"I can handle him," was the reply.

"That's what you think," Leroy told Jimmy. "He's not the same racer when he gets Down Under."

Davies' record would have been much different had he not heeded Warriner's warning.

The second year Davies took even more equipment with him and the two superstars were joined by 1952 National Midget Champion, Johnnie Tolan. Tolan, like Davies, had raced at Indianapolis and enjoyed plenty of midget success at the peak of his career, but when he came to Australia he was in the latter part of his racing days.

Tolan had the Kischell Offy, Tat the Mattoon car and Davies brought a car reputed to have been raced previously by Allen Heath.

It was not a happy tour for Tolan who finished the campaign in the hospital after a crash at the Sydney Showground.

In 1965 Tat had the blue and white #54 Hollywood Spring and Axle car with him. At the completion of the tour it was sold to Australian driver, Barry Valentinna.

The next year Tat was accompanied by Californian, Sherman Cleveland, who was an aggressive campaigner. He sent the Australian fans into a frenzy at almost every venue he raced. Empire Speedways wanted the big attraction back again. Shortly before leaving Australia, Cleveland agreed to terms for a return visit.

Bob Tattersall already had his opinion of Cleveland.

A driver full of courage, Tat believed he was a little too brave and told Mr. Sherwood that Cleveland would either go on and become a brilliant midget driver or the contract would never be fulfilled.

Tat's chilling prediction proved correct. Cleveland did not meet the return agreement. He was killed in a sprint car later that year at Calistoga, California.

In 1967 Tat brought to Australia the then current USAC National Midget Champion, Mike McGreevy, and what an introduction he had to Australian racing!

First night out at the Sydney Showground firey Kiwi driver, Barry Butterworth was disqualified during the main event. When Butterworth refused to quit the race the event was stopped and a near riot broke out. Hundreds of fans jumped the fence and staged a "sit in" on the track. Police were called in to restore order. Butterworth was reinstated at the request of the police, and when the race resumed, it was Tattersall who gave them all a driving lesson. "Iron Mike" McGreevy finished second on that long remembered hot summer night at the Showground in February of 1967.

The next year Californian, Don Meacham and Billy Mehner, from Portland, Oregon, raced in Australia with Tat. Both were a big hit with the fans.

In 1968 Tat had the Kischell Offy — raced in Australia in 1964 by Tolan — but the tour was full of frustration for The Streator Streak. A succession of engine failures kept his winning aggregate down.

In 1969 Tat raced the ex-Meacham car which had been purchased by Don Mackay. Mackay and Tattersall proved an almost unbeatable combination and it was one of Tat's most successful Australian tours.

(Top) **Tat #3 chases Peter Cunneen #4 and Ken Morton #77 at the Sydney Showground in 1963.** *Larry Taylor photo. Nunn Collection.*
(Bottom) **Jeff Freeman #75 in the Mackay Offy and Tat in the #3 Mattoon Imperial Motors Offy at the Showground in 1963.** *Larry Taylor photo. Nunn Collection.*

(Top) Howard Revell #2 in the Berco Holden and Tat #76 in the Mackay Offy at the Sydney Showground 1969. *Ian Smith photo. Nunn Collection.*
(Bottom) Bill Mehner #63 and Sid Middlemass #54 are challenged by Tat #12. *Ian Smith photo. Nunn Collection.*

(Top) Sherman Cleveland #10 poses with Tat #35 at the Showground in 1966. *Ian Smith photo. Nunn Collection.*
(Bottom) Bob Tattersall in Jack Stroud's Honker Down Under. *Ian Smith photo. Nunn Collection.*

As cold water to a thirsty soul, so is good news from a far country. Proverbs 25:25.

14

New Zealand

A thousand miles to the east of Australia and overshadowed in size are two islands that make up New Zealand. Called the Britain of the South because of the striking resemblances to England, the 1200 mile long country has seen speedcar activity mainly in Auckland located at the north end of North Island.

Like its Australian neighbor, the Kiwis haven't missed out when it comes to midget race car competition.

Frank "Satan" Brewer, whose name crops up all over this book, won the first of three New Zealand Championships in 1940.

When the New Zealand promoters heard about the American, Bob Tattersall, and what he was doing in Australia, they wanted him to appear at their Western Springs track.

Western Springs and Claremont on the West Coast of Australia shared more in common than the tracks on the east side of Australia, both were miles from the other tracks. As a result Tat would have to fly to these tracks and race a local car or schedule his appearances to coincide with his trips to Australia by boat.

When Tat was in town the fans would come early to the Western Springs track to watch him warm-up. The track had a cement velodrome bicycle track built around the dirt surface used for the speedcars and Tat used the banked track for warm-ups pretending he was at Winchester or Salem, Indiana.

Two New Zealand drivers who raced in America with the USAC stars were Barry Handlin and Trevor Morris.

If Tat raced in New Zealand before going to Australia, and was beaten, the Australians knew he would take it out on them, so they cheered for Tat when he was at Auckland.

Most racers would give their eye teeth to have the record Bob Tattersall set in Kiwi Country.

He raced there on 38 different occasions, competing in 143 races. Out of these he had 41 firsts, 18 seconds and 11 third place finishes. In 31 races he retired either through accident or mechanical failure.

Out of 30 feature races he was first 22 times, second three times and third three times. He won the World Quarter Mile Track Championship in 1966-67, spun out in the 1967-68 race and won the title again in 1968-69. The following year he placed second.

Tat truly was King in three countries.

NEW ZEALAND RECORD

38 Events

# Races	1st	2nd	3rd	4th	cr/fil	bal
143	41	18	11	1	31	41= 143

FEATURE

RACES	1st	2nd	3rd	4th	other
30	22	3	3	1	1= 30

(Top) A drawing by Gordon McIsaac of Jeff Freeman running over the top of Tat during a race at Western Springs Speedway. Tat won the 1965 event with Jeff placing second.
(Bottom) Tat's #54 carries the scars from the Jeff Freeman incident.
Ian Smith photo.

To everything there is a season, and a time for every matter or purpose under heaven. Ecclesiastes 3:1.

15

Kings Cross

During his years in Australia Tat cemented many friendships — friendships which lasted right to the end of his life.

In Sydney, the McGee family was heavily involved with his race campaign. It all started in 1960 when Tat brought the Saylor Offy to the Sydney Showground. Hedley McGee was the head of the McGee Racing Cams operation and his workshop in Sydney's Kings Cross was a speedway landmark. It was the stopping off point for many out of town race drivers. Hedley was already involved in midget racing when Tat first came to Sydney and so it seemed only natural that Bob, like many other visitors, would house his car at the McGee garage.

As the sixties unfolded the fame of the garage grew as Tattersall became a national figure. People would drive for miles to see the workplace of Australia's great sports figure. Hedley's eldest son, Phil, later became Tat's crew chief.

"My family had been housing U.S. race cars for some time, so it was only natural for Bob to stay at the nearby Bernleigh Hotel and literally walk to our workshop to prepare his car," Phil explained.

The McGee Racing Cams Company operated out of an area of Sydney which was noted for its night clubs, strip joints, gambling houses and bars. For speedway people the general meeting place was the nearby Greenpark Hotel, an establishment Bob Tattersall regularly frequented.

The Greenpark Hotel was where the Sydney speedcar fraternity met to make new rules, increase horsepower, lie about gear ratios, figure out the ultimate chassis setup or tell Tattersall they were catching up to him or running right with him after he'd lapped some of them two or three times.

Phil McGee's involvement with Tat commenced with the 1960 season. Hedley told his teenage son to stay away from the newest American. Of course Phil became curious and fascinated with the rough talking Tattersall.

"One winter he brought the Cascio Offy over to our house at Coogee and asked us to rebuild it for him as he had sold it to Empire Speedways. I was grateful to have the opportunity to work on such a car after I had spent years watching my dad fix bent race cars."

"On his return trip from the States, Tat brought the hard parts (crankshaft, etc.) to finish the project. This started one of the best friendships of my life," Phil McGee said.

In those initial years, Phil was restricted to building Bob's engines and general maintenance. It was several more years before Phil accompanied Tat on the full campaign throughout Australia.

Tat wasn't lonely during those early years. Barry Rainbow ran a cab company and a wrecker service. In the early years Barry was hired to transport Tat's race car. Once he got hooked up with the "cowboy" he forgot about business. His mom would call the bachelor and tell him to come home. He'd tell her "OK" and keep right on going. One time he stayed with Tat and Dee during the entire tour. Barry also made it to New Zealand to help out with both the race car and the parties. Allen Borgman, Howard Powers and Peter Nunn also helped entertain the visiting hero.

Phil had a front row seat to some of the most amusing incidents that clearly underline why Bob Tattersall became such a colourful character in Australia.

"The stories that came back to me about Bob's antics were nothing short of unbelievable," relates Phil McGee. Like the time he went to a party after a successful night at Rowley Park in South Australia. He went with a group of friends including Ross Turner, a well-known jockey. The story goes that a friend of Turner was showing off with a revolver and started waving it around. Bob relieved this gentleman of his weapon and fired it at a painting on the wall. He didn't hit the painting. He hit the nail that was hanging the picture, driving it into the wall and sending the framed work crashing to the floor.

Of course, everyone at the party thought this was intentional and treated Tattersall with great respect. They now knew this "cowboy" from Streator, Illinois, could not only drive race cars, but was also a crack shot.

Bob later told Phil privately that he could not have done that again if he fired a hundred rounds. Phil doubts that anyone there has ever forgotten what they saw.

One night in Perth, West Australia, Bob had been out drinking with some of the local cops and later got apprehended for drunk-driving as he made his way back to the motel. Bob thought these were the same cops he'd been with earlier and let loose with the famous Tattersall barrage of verbal abuse, calling them everything, and more. The police arrested him and put him in the lockup overnight.

Eventually everything was straightened out with the judge, who just happened to be a fan and devoted follower of Bob Tattersall.

Americans know football players. Australians in the 60's knew Tat.

Leroy Warriner remembers a night when a group threw a party for Tat and he didn't arrive. That didn't stop the party which was going strong when the guest finally appeared in the wee hours of the morning. "Hi everyone," shouted Tat with a big wave. He then passed out.

The 1968 season with the Kischell Offy was a frustrating time for both Bob and Phil McGee. The Kischell Offy was lightning fast while the engine stayed together, but keeping the Offy that way wasn't working out. Tat had countless races "in the bag" only to have the engine blow to pieces.

The seriousness of the tour did have its lighter moments as related by Phil.

"I flew from Sydney to Adelaide to work on the car. Most of the parts had been thrashed and while waiting for Don Kischell to send more parts, we pieced together what was basically the motor from our McGee Offy."

"We checked into a motel near the race track and I went to the office to find out when the daily dry cleaning service came by."

"While I was at the office the dry cleaning girl was already there to pick up Bob's Hinchman uniform."

"She knocked on the door. Believing it was me, Bob stepped out of the shower and answered the door stark naked. By this time I had neared the room and knew what had happened when I heard the scream."

"By the time I arrived she had composed herself. She even asked Bob for his autograph."

It wasn't just engines Bob had trouble with. He called home to Paul Baines one year and told him to send another "filing block" for the Offy. The unit is used to hand file Offy valves. "What's the matter with the one you have?" asked Baines.

About that time Kym Bonython got on the phone and related how Tat had not wiped off the table and the filing block was sitting on a pile of shavings. When Tat tried to use it, it rocked back and forth. Seems he threw it clear across the street and through a plate glass window of a store.

During the Australian tour after winning the USAC National Championship Tat was burned on his lower legs. Phil remembers Tat getting burned two weeks running in what amounted to burns over burns.

After the races Phil took him to the local hospital. He was really in pain. The doctor explained to him the severity of the burns and the risk of infection and warned him not to get his wounds wet. That same night the gang was having a pool party at the Roy Sands Motel in Adelaide. Bob was nowhere to be found. Then all of a sudden, Tat jumped off the motel roof wearing a towel around his shoulders and plastic bags over his legs and feet. He just about emptied the pool when he splashed down, soaking everyone, including some guests who were not race fans.

Bob made friends, meeting new people everywhere he went, and people from all walks of life. Many of his trips were by ship. He was a good paratrooper because he did not like flying and the three week ocean voyage was very relaxing after a hectic racing season in America.

He partied as hard on the ships as he did in Australia and on one occasion brought most of the crew from the ship to the Showground to watch him race...and party afterwards.

The partying afterwards continued outside the Showground in "Driver Avenue" which involved drivers and the general racing fraternity. Bob was in his element.

The gatherings after the race became almost as famous as the ontrack action by the world's best in both bikes and cars.

Bob would leave early if there was work to do on the car. Racing and winning always came first. Good preparation usually allowed him time to party after the race into the wee hours of the morning.

Phil's dad, Hedley, had a good sense of humour and got the best of Tat frequently. During one Christmas gathering in the earlier years, Hedley told Tat to watch his language in front of the kids. Bob replied, "Sure, Hedley. I haven't said %*X**% all day."

"You can trust me."

Then a little later in the day Hedley was talking about another driver and Bob interrupted, "That **%@*&**. He's no good you know."

"He only brings s... boxes over here to sell."

Hedley said, "That's it. I told you not to use that kind of language in my house. I won't let you come here again!"

Hedley was only joking but Bob took him seriously. As it happened the McGee gatherings were off for the next couple of years because they were too busy racing. Poor Bob really believed he had been kept out of the fun.

Later when Bob was invited to a mid-week dinner with the family he became very emotional and thanked Hedley for giving him another chance. Then Hedley explained that Bob had been on the receiving end of a good joke.

The association Bob Tattersall enjoyed with Empire Speedways had a spin-off affect in other areas. Empire's Frank Arthur had made it a practice to name young horses after winners of his international midget events at either Sydney or Brisbane. The first was named "Warriner" and it won a couple of races in Queensland country before it was sold to interests in North Queensland.

Then Frank Arthur named the next horse "Tattersall."

It did not take long for this horse to uphold the reputation of his namesake. In Brisbane, on Wednesday evening October 29, 1963, the headline in the sporting pages of a local daily newspaper read:

SPEEDWAY PROMOTER A WINNER

Thus announcing the success of a horse named "Tattersall," who had won his first race with an impressive performance which had turf writers knocking out superlatives in their coverage of the event.

Ironically, "Tattersall" won his first race eight years to the day Bob Tattersall was laid to rest.

(Top) **Bruce Barnes watches as Tat entices Jeff Freeman.** *Bruce Kent photo.*
(Below) **Merle Bettenhausen and Tat.** *Dee Tattersall Collection.*

(*Top*) **Tat #35 in the Stroud Offy leads John Stewart #1 in the McGee Holden at the Sydney Showground** *Ian Smith photo. Nunn Collection.*
(*Bottom*) **Barry Butterworth #7 Mackay Offy with Tat #12 in the Kischell Offy.** *Ian Smith photo. Nunn Collection.*

(Top) Bob Tattersall in the Mackay Offy #76 in 1969. *Ian Smith photo. Nunn Collection.*
(Bottom) L to R. Bob Tattersall, Merle Bettenhausen and John Stewart.
Ian Smith photo. Nunn Collection.

A man who hath friends must show himself friendly; and there is a friend who sticketh closer than a brother. Proverbs 18:24.

16

Friends

Bob Tattersall had hundreds of friends, however, there were those special friends, the ones that stick closer than a brother.

Wild Willie Wildhaber would always be close. Tat could count on Frank Barsi. Howard Powers would be extra special.

Just how Tat and Powers became such close friends remains a hidden part of the legend. Howard ran his own catering and canteen service. He was an accomplished pilot and a bit of a daredevil. Once the air show stunt pilot got involved with Bob Tattersall he was never the same. After one season with Tat, he proclaimed himself, "Bob Tattersall's Chief Goggle Washer."

What made the relationship so strange was that, like Kym Bonython, Howard did not drink.

In Howard Powers, Tat had found not only his Australian Willie Wildhaber, but a chauffeur and caretaker also.

From that year on, when Tat came to Australia, Howard quit whatever he was doing and traveled with his new friend.

The two loved to go water skiing and one time showed their stuff by both skiing on just one ski together.

The women got along fine, but after a couple of seasons Howard's wife wondered how Dee could put up with it all.

There exists a movie of the "two terrors" on a train. The club car is full of women attracted to the American hero and his friend. Of course they were all Howard's women when Tat brought the film home and showed it to Dee.

Race drivers learn early that having fellow drivers as close friends can hurt. In the years Tat raced, death would always be around. When someone close died it brought back memories of six-year-old Billy.

Joking and fooling around was OK, just don't get too close.

Tat did get close to several drivers. One was an Australian named Jeff Freeman. Another was his old IMCA buddy, Bobby Grim.

Just after Tat got home from his first trip to the land of kangaroos, in the spring of 1959 Bobby Grim raced in his first Indianapolis 500 Mile Race. Bobby was named the Rookie of the Year. In that race he had thrown up his hand to warn of a four car crash and the wind, at high speed, had dislocated his shoulder. He drove another forty laps before the car quit.

In 1959 Bobby Grim drove in twelve USAC Midget races. Tat ran eight.

After the 1960 season in Australia, Tat was ready to race in USAC on a full time basis. In his first shot at the tough Championship he competed in forty-four races. Jimmy Davies raced in fifty-five events and won the first of three titles. Bobby Grim ran his second Indy 500 and ran twenty-one midget events.

Soon the Tattersalls and the Grims were sharing their homes with each other. When the USAC races were up north the Grims could always stay with Bob and Dee. The same was true for the Tattersalls when the races were around Indy.

In the interwoven lives of racing people the story of the Grims and the Tattersalls would blend from one generation to another.[14]

A few years back Bob Tattersall had broken Frankie Luptow's "Australian Pursuit" record during an IMCA sprint car race.

Luptow had been killed in a stock car in 1952. Bobby Grim had married his widow in 1954 and raised his daughter, Susie. She would share a life with one Jimmy Caruthers ten years into the future.

Jimmy Caruthers would be tutored by Robert George Tattersall and would become a USAC Champion.

In Australia in 1960, Jeff Freeman would begin a tutoring under the wing of the same Robert George Tattersall.

Jeff was a young talented speedcar driver from the Sydney suburb of Paddington. Like Tat, he was popular and had charisma. Jeff loved the fans and learned to do sign language so he could communicate with the deaf after being confronted with a group of such fans.

Tat took a liking to the young Aussie and decided to teach him not only the fine art of race car driving, but how to win at drinking scotch and how to party.

Jeff learned to party, but like many of Tat's closest friends, drinking didn't suit him. For Jeff a couple of beers was enough.

In Brisbane the pair would stay...make that..."take over" the Beachcomber Hotel despite the pleadings of the manager not to throw anyone into the swimming pool, which usually got him thrown in, clothes and all.

When Tat had buzzed the Royale in Tony Saylor's car, every owner in Australia and New Zealand wanted one like it. Don Mackay purchased two and signed Jeff

[14]The continuing story is captured in Hal Higdon's "Summer Of Triumph, ©1977, published by G.P. Putnam.

Freeman as one of his drivers.

The five years of friendship between the youngster and the teacher was highlighted in 1965.

Eric Kydd, the head of the maintenance division of Qantas Air Lines became the chief mechanic of Jeff Freeman's car. He also had a new creation under way for the man he considered the best Australian driver racing at that time.

The second Mackay car was not working and veteran, Len Brock, lost his ride to Nick Collier. Collier was so ecstatic that he told a friend, "I think I've reached my high point in Speedway, I now have a ride in an Offy."

The first race in the car was uneventful. The second race he finished seventh and then he won the third. His fourth race was on February 27, 1965.

Bob Tattersall was in town and Nick Collier by virtue of his feature win the race before, would get a chance to go up against Tat in a try for the track record.

Tat went first and in typical Two Gun style, stopped the clock at 19 seconds, matching the existing record held by himself, Len Brock and Jeff Freeman.

Next it was Collier's turn.

For the first time with real power, Nick rang the rafters with an 18-9/10 clocking. Tat had been beaten by the Tony Saylor Offy he had sold after the fantastic 1960 season, and which now belonged to Mackay.

In the feature, Freeman shot to the front from sixteenth starting position. Tat, started eighteenth and was slower through traffic. Collier struggled from fourteenth.

By the time Tat got into second, Freeman was gone and the old pro had to settle for second place.

People had already started to leave when Collier ran over the wheel of a lapped car as he finished the race.

He suffered head injuries in the crash. At 1:30 a.m. he died in the local hospital.

Ironically, a close friend and pit man to Len Brock, Harry Pfahl, was emotionally affected by the crash and lost his life in a head-on crash on his way home from the track.

Jeff continued his form in what has been called the greatest midget race ever run in Australia, the 1965 Grand Prix.

It was the only time in the thirteen years Tat raced Down Under that a driver who started behind him, passed him to win.

In the next big event, Bob Tattersall had his hands full as he won his fourth World Speedcar Championship with his protege, Jeff Freeman, right behind at the finish.

***

On Saturday, May 8, 1965, Bob and Dee Tattersall went on a shopping spree in Jeffersonville, Indiana, to find gifts for their mothers. Tomorrow they would drive to Seneca and celebrate Mother's Day with Mom Tattersall.

Around midnight they were on their way home from Tat's second USAC midget race of the season. Tat was not pleased with ninth quick time and an eleventh in the feature.

"Just couldn't get going tonight. Just didn't feel right."

In Westmead, Australia, it was already Mother's Day and Jeff Freeman had just charged from fifteenth starting position to fourth place on the half-mile dirt track.

Rain had left the track quite muddy and a grader had shoved the heavy mud to the outside, up against the fence.

It was Jeff who had warned the other drivers not to get up high or they would be in trouble.

On the fifth lap the right rear tire of the black and gold number 75 struck the dangerous ridge of mud. When the cartwheeling machine had come to rest, Jeffrey Edwin Freeman, age 27, was gone.

***

In July, Australia lost Tony Burke who fought to live for six days after his crash at Westmead.

At the moment of death, Bob Tattersall was winning his eighth USAC feature.

The show goes on. That's the way it is!

Post script: 1500 people attended Jeff Freeman's funeral. Don Mackay was devastated by the loss of his second driver in one year. Eric Kydd rebuilt the #75 and it raced again as the E.J. Kydd Offy. Kydd did not finish the car he was building for Jeff Freeman until 1974, nine years after his death.

The car has never been raced.[15]

***

After Jeff Freeman's death the deaf fans almost stopped attending the races. In 1967 after beating Johnny Stewart, Freeman's arch rival, in the World Derby, Tat was approached by the group. They had returned to the track to see Bob because they knew he and Jeff were friends. When Bob saw them using two hands to communicate he asked who they were. He then shocked everyone by talking to them in sign language using one hand. They joined Tat and Peter Nunn in front of the speedway, a place where the parties usually started, and Tat stayed and talked with them late into the morning.

It seemed that Bob's grandmother was deaf and so Tat learned the language as a boy. These fans had a new hero and Tat had more friends.

***

[15]The above information was compiled from stories by Bill Lawler and Dennis Newlyn, Speedway Classics #3.

Friends

Bobby Grim was well respected around the Indianapolis Motor Speedway. He had talked his friend, Bob Tattersall, into spending time at Indy.

"This is where the money is you fool. A good finish here is worth more than you make all year."

The biggest problem a Speedway Rookie has is getting someone to give him a ride so he can take the mandatory driver's test.

Gary Bettenhausen had found a ride in an old Dan Gurney Eagle owned by Dave McManus. The car hadn't made a race on the circuit and Gary was just starting his fourth year as a race driver.

When the USAC officials told Gary he needed more experience before trying Indianapolis, Bobby Grim saw a chance for Bob Tattersall to take his driver's test in the car.

The old Eagle was a piece of junk, as the remainder of the season proved, and Bob Tattersall was a nervous wreck.

If you messed up at Indy, everyone in the world knew it. The race track had the wrong surface and the car had the engine on the wrong end. There's pressure everywhere, mostly from yourself.

The speed wasn't a problem. Bob had run close to 150 in a midget and a high 158 average would make the race.

Like a figure skater under the watchful eyes of many judges, the driver must perform to get certified for Indy.

Tat was so nervous he wouldn't go out by the track without Bobby Grim beside him. Like an under age kid sitting in a bar, he was certain that everyone at Indy was watching him.

"Bobby Grim to the garage please," barked the PA.

When Grim got to the garage Tat was trying to put a new set of lenses into his goggles. "Where the heck is Howard Powers when you need him?"

Grim took the goggles from the shaking hands and inserted the plastic lenses into the rubber.

"Lighten up old buddy. You're just going to run ten laps."

Once Tat was on the track, Grim decided to try and settle him down. Taking a brand new chalk board he wrote SCREW YOU in big bold letters, using the four letter version of the phrase.

After showing the board to Tat, Bobby wiped it off and leaned it up against the wall that separates the inside of the track from the pits.

Bobby didn't realize that a new black board will show what was written on it after it is erased. Laughter and cheers from the few hundred people in the seats behind the pit called his attention to the fact.

The clutch went out of the car with one phase left on Tat's test. Grim found another car for him to use, but Harlan Fengler, the chief steward for the race, decided to make a new rule.

"He'll have to complete the test in the car he started in."

Bobby recruited nine guys to help push the car so Tat could jam it into high gear and run the last ten lap phase.

Wed May 18, 1966.

Driver testing was another big item of the day with three drivers completing their test receiving the blessings of the veterans driving committee. Larry Dickson in the Mitchner Petroleum Special #34, Ronnie Bucknum in the Arciero Special #69 and Bob Tattersall in the McManus #61. This brought to end the 1966 test period for rookie drivers with a total of fifteen complete tests.

Those passing the four phases are Art Pollard, Jackie Stewart, Bob Hurt, Greg Weld, Gary Congdon, Cale Yarborough, Gig Stevens, Sam Sessions, Dick Atkins, Lee Roy Yarbrough, Red Regal,

Bruce Jacobi, Larry Dickson, Ronnie Bucknum, and Bob Tattersall.

Passing the refresher course were Mike McGreevy, Carl Williams, Mel Kenyon, Graham Hill, and Ralph Ligouri.[16]

Eight drivers in the 1966 Rookie Class never drove in the race. Only seven were able to place in the top ten. Graham Hill won the 500 in '66 as a rookie. Gary Congdon qualified but crashed on the first lap and, later that fall, was killed at the Terre Haute Action Track during the "Hut 100." Dick Atkins did not make the field and died along with Don Branson in November at Ascot Park during a Sprint Car Race. Bob Hurt was paralyzed in a crash at the Speedway in 1968 —he never made the race. Sam Sessions best finish was 1972 when he was fourth; he died racing snowmobiles in 1977. Art Pollard became a favorite of the Speedway fans; he died at the Speedway in 1973. Mike McGreevy won his second USAC Midget Championship in 1966 without racing at Indianapolis; he went to Australia with Tat and now lives in Florida where he breeds race horses. Mel Kenyon raced at Indy eight times placing 3rd once, 4th twice and 5th once; he went on to be USAC Midget Champion seven times and holds the record for all-time midget victories. Ralph "Cousin" Ligouri became the oldest rookie at Indy as he tried and tried again; he never made the race and continues to run midgets. Larry Dickson won in the dangerous Sprint Cars as USAC Champion; he raced at Indy eight times placing 8th in 1969. Jackie Stewart, the Formula One Champion, placed 6th his rookie year. Greg Weld did not make the race until 1970, placing 32nd. Cale Yarborough made four races. Lee Roy Yarbrough ran Indy three times. The two NASCAR stars saw Bruce Jacobi try the stocks after failing Indy...he was paralyzed in a crash at Daytona in 1983 and died in 1987. Ronnie Bucknum's best of three races was 15th in 1970. Carl Williams was 9th that same year and died in 1973. Gig Stevens and Red Regal crashed during practice. They never made the race. Regal and Jud Larson died twelve days after Indy in a crash at Reading.

Bob Tattersall won the USAC Midget Championship and was "King of Down Under" until his death.

Chuck Rodee, a top midget driver, was trying for his third 500 in 1966 when he crashed in a qualifying attempt and was killed. Two-time winner, Rodger Ward had crashed the same car the year before and missed the show. He retired in 1966 after placing 15th, saying, "It just isn't fun anymore."

Tat missed the show at Trenton in 1965 in his only ride in a roadster. After passing his rookie test in 1966 he raced Carl Gehlhausen's #84 Championship Dirt Car in four different races. His other appearances showed him as a "did not start" at the Hoosier Hundred in 1960 for Harry Turner and Bob giving up his ride to Parnelli Jones at Langhorn in 1963 where Parnelli placed 4th. His last time in a Championship car was April 23, 1967 in Jake Vargo's Offy at Trenton, New Jersey where he placed tenth.

Bob Tattersall thought driving an Indy Car was like "Passing wind against thunder." The opportunity at Indy never happened, but he did work as a mechanic in the Gene White stable in 1968 and saw Lloyd Ruby finish 5th and Bobby Grim duplicate his 1964 tenth place finish.

Missing Indy never really bothered Tat that much. In 1967 he went to Indianapolis planning to look for a ride. That was when his kidney acted up. Grim took him to "Methodist," the hospital of the racers.

"Tat, we've found a tumor in one of your kidneys. It's cancerous and will have to come out."

The operation went well. Few of the racers knew

about the cancer, but they knew Tat had been through major surgery.

"I know it's race time," the doctor lectured, "but I don't want you out riding around in a car."

As Bobby was driving Tat back to the house from the hospital he remarked, "You know, it's about time for me to trade this old clunker off."

When Tat was settled in, Bobby disappeared. Several hours later he came driving up in a new Ford Ranchero.

"Doc didn't say anything about a truck, did he?"

Tat and Bobby ran all over Indy in the new vehicle, but the doctor would not release him to race for six weeks.

George Tattersall was shaken by Tat's illness and had come to Indianapolis to be with his son. George had quit drinking but along with the worry came the urge to go back to the bottle.

The Grim's had gone beyond friendship when Tat was released from Methodist. He had gone through morphine withdrawal, which was an ordeal on the entire household, as well as Tat.

When it was noticed that the Grims' bar was being depleted at a rapid rate, George's drinking was discovered. It was decided that the best thing would be to send him home on the bus.

A few days after he got home, Tat's father went fishing. He was struck and killed by a car while on his way home.

Bob and Dee weren't able to make the trip home for the funeral and it was really a hard time in their lives.

Bob felt responsible just as he had with Billy, and his sister Kathryn.

Tat had signed with Jack Stroud to drive the brand new Honker II midget. Both men wanted to win the National Championship and realized that with the hospital stay it would not be this year. Jack Stroud waited for his driver to get well.

The first race after the hospital was at Hershey, Pennsylvania on July 14th. With sixth fastest time and third in the heat, Stroud knew Tat had not lost his touch.

On the start of the feature Tat moved to the outside and charged. Going thru turns one and two he passed cars from his thirteenth starting position.

"BOB TATTERSALL'S FLIPPING DOWN THE BACKSTRETCH," the announcer screamed into the mike.

Bob Tattersall was back!

"Same old Tat!"

"Hasn't lost a thing!"

L to R. Dee, Jeff Freeman, Jeff's girl friend, Doreen and Tat at the Sydney Airport March 29, 1964. *Dee Tattersall Collection.*

(Center) Tat and Jeff Freeman.
(Lower Left) Tat and Jeff Freeman's mother. Taken a year after his death. *Dee Tattersall Collection.*
(Lower Right) Jeff Freeman in the Hollywood Spring and Axle car in Auckland, NZ. 1965. *Bruce Kent photo.*

(Top) **Bob Tattersall during his Indianapolis Rookie Test in 1966.**
Dee Tattersall Collection.
(Below) **Tat's only time in an Indianapolis Roadster at Trenton, New Jersey.**
Dee Tattersall Collection.

(Top) Lloyd Ruby's 1968 Indy crew. Tat is behind Ruby on the right and was the engine man on the 5th place car. *Dee Tattersall Collection.*
(Below) L to R. Shorty Templeman, Jack Turner, and Chuck Rodee in the "Indy Cafe." *Ed Hitze photo.*

Tat in the Mid West Mfg. Championship Dirt car at Sacramento, CA in 1966.
Dee Tattersall Collection.

Know you not that they who run in a race all run, but one receiveth the prize? So run that you might obtain.
I Corinthians 9:24.

17

The Prize

"Will I ever win the Championship?" wondered Tat. Mel Kenyon and Mike McGreevy had been the top dogs for five years. The race schedule had been over fifty races long, dropping to forty-nine in 1967. The hospital stay had taken care of that year. Each year it was the number of races that made a big difference. In 1964 he had run ten less than Kenyon and placed 7th. In 1965 he ran three races less than McGreevy and won twelve features to Mike's seven and still wound up 2nd. In '66 he was down nine races and placed 4th, in '67 the shortage was sixteen and again he was 4th.

The schedule was way up in 1968. Mel Kenyon ran fifty-nine races. Tat ran thirty-eight and managed to place 3rd.

In midget racing it is not only the nightly purse that counts. Winning the Championship pays in two ways. First there is the point fund which is paid by the promoters on top of the purse. Placing high in the points pays a huge bonus at the end of the year. Then there is the Championship money paid by the promoters the following year.

In the 60's it was fifty dollars paid to the Defending Champion provided he participated in your event.

With a seventy race schedule this amounted to $3,500

a season to a team. The top drivers in the point standings were only winning fourteen to seventeen thousand dollars a season, so the Champion's fee equaled a fourth of the winnings.

In 1969 the midgets had come back into the limelight. The Houston Astrodome would build a quarter mile race track inside the massive facility and race for two days. The entire purse would be $63,000.

Tat's coming home early!

2/12/69: Quip of the week: An ARDC midget mechanic upon learning that Bob Tattersall was returning from Australia to run in USAC's $50,000 Astrodome midget meet on March 8th and 9th said, "For a $5,000 purse he runs over you. For $50,000 he'll probably run through you.[17]

The prediction never got a chance. Car trouble left the best driver in Australia with a slow qualifying time and for two days of racing the Honker II crew could only show one win in a heat race.

Tattersall did make news while in Houston. Midget racing had a new safety device which would spark controversy all year. The Kenyon brothers 3-K Racing and Howard Linne's shops were the main suppliers of the Edmunds Chassis as well as other racing parts including the 110 Offy Engine and the new Sesco Chevy. The new item was the roll cage which should make midgets a lot safer, especially when they got upside down.

Naturally one would expect the "King of Upside Down" to have one on his car.

Bob Tattersall had run many races for Howard Linne and Linne had given him a ride during his early USAC career. It was Linne who would supply Tat a car whenever his regular ride had trouble. Tat had also done a great deal of testing on the new Sesco, which puked oil like a new baby on solid food for the first time.

[17]Chris Economaki. From the editor's desk. Speed Sport News.

Tat agreed to try a cage at the Astrodome. "Hey, Stroud. As long as we're hanging all these bars on the car, why not put a wing on it?"

After checking the rule book the pair thought they had a great idea. The competition didn't think so and Jack Stroud along with the other two owners who tried it were forced to remove the tin on top.

After missing the show and with all the fuss over the wings, Tat told Jack to ditch the cage. From that moment on he was against them.

"They make bad drivers brave," stated Tat. "You've got guys running ten miles an hour over their heads!"

With the interest the Astrodome race brought to midget racing, the USAC schedule had increased to a record seventy-seven races. Only four races had been run before the Astrodome and Mel Kenyon had placed in the top four once. Tat would have his best shot ever at the National Championship.

One habit Tat had in the past was to come to the pits when the car was not working rather than stay in the race and finish poorly. This year Tat was out for all the points he could get. No matter what, he stayed out there.

Les Scott beat Kenyon at Tucson with Tat fourth. Kenyon won Phoenix with Tat second. Mel was second to McGreevy at Fresno and Tat hung on to fifteenth place.

At Hershey, Pennsylvania Tat and Kenyon started up front with Les Scott right behind them. Tat took the lead and Kenyon poked his nose up beside the Streator driver twice.

Les Scott tells the rest of the story best:

Kenyon came up on Tat twice and Tat just let him go. I was working better than Tat and I put a nose on him. He slammed the door on me and crowded the inside of the flat track. The rest of the race I bumped, hammered and pushed all over him and he never let me by. When we got done he had tire marks all over the tail of the Honker II.[18]

The next day the tour went to Jennerstown and when Dee got out of the car she walked up to Polly Scott. "Is it OK if I sit with you? I'm not on your list am I?" asked Dee.

"No, we're not mad at you," replied Polly.

About that time Tat hollered at Les, "Hey Les, how about coming over here and helping me wash off all these tire marks?"

Tat won at Jennerstown and again at Davenport, Iowa. Santa Fe and IRP were both bad, followed by a fifth place at both Kokomo, Indiana and Rockford, Illinois.

In June of 1969 Mel was on a hot streak. He had placed fourth in the Indianapolis 500 and was out to win his fourth Midget Championship.

Tat was second at Avilla and sixth at Jackson, Michigan, which were both won by Mel Kenyon.

In Lansing, Michigan, Kenyon's luck turned. Lansing was a paved quarter mile track with the pits located at the end of the main straightaway. To get to the pits, you drove down the main straightaway and through the gate, then turned right into the pit area.

When you drove off the track you were facing a cement wall that required you to turn right a second time.

At the start of the race the pit gate was left open. Mel, on the outside, bumped wheels with another car just past the starting line. His car was forced out against the fence.

Had he tried to make the first turn he would have hit the end of the retaining wall.

Without thinking Mel flew thru the opened gate. His car went airborne as it went over the hump.

---

[18]Les Scott, USAC Driver. **162**

The race was red flagged and everyone rushed to the pits.

Mel's car had landed before he hit the cement wall in the pits, but still traveling nearly seventy miles an hour, Mel had pitched the car sideways and sailed into the concrete.

The sides of the tires gripped the wall and the car literally stopped on a dime.

Mel was conscious but the crash knocked the wind out of him. The medics struggled to get him breathing again.

The car looked to be ok. There wasn't a scratch on it, but later, Mel and Don began to magniflux the car and found that every piece of the car was cracked. The frame, motor mounts, wheels, rear end, steering, even the motor block was cracked like the shell of a hard boiled egg that was used for a football.

Three days after Lansing, the midgets ran at Davenport, Iowa. Bob Tattersall won the feature. The next night was Madison, Wisconsin.

Howard Linne had offered Mel a ride in his second car while Mel and Don were building a new machine to replace the wrecked one.

At Madison the race for points became highlighted. The track was a well banked paved oval. The grandstand was built into a hillside and the scoring tower was well behind the grandstand. The yellow and green track lights were operated from a panel of light switches similar to those you have in your home. There was a third switch which operated a light over the flag stand to tell the flagman when to throw the white flag.

Everything went fine that night until the end of the feature race.

What a race it was!

Mel Kenyon was leading Henry Pens in a hot battle. Pens was Howard Linne's top driver and Mel was in

Linne's other car. Pens tried time after time to get by Mel.

Near the end of the feature Johnny Shipman, the flagman, began to look up to the booth for Les Kimbrell's signal to throw the white flag.

As Kenyon led Pens across the line completing twenty-eight laps, Les reached for the light switch to signal Shipman.

The moment he threw it, Les knew it was the wrong switch!

The yellow light flashed on and one driver in the pack raised his hand and slowed down.

Les immediately switched off the yellow and looked for the right switch, but by the time he threw the correct one, Mel and Pens had crossed the line on what was supposed to be the white flag lap.

As the cars came to the line for what should have been the checkered flag they received the white flag telling them they had one more lap to go.

Henry Pens let it all hang out in the last turn, squeaked under Kenyon and took the checkered flag.

As he received the trophy Howard Linne was ecstatic.

Mel and Don Kenyon knew racing and Don suspected that the race had gone over the required laps. The rule book stated that a race was over when either the required distance or the checkered flag was displayed, so the Kenyon's protested the race.

Howard Linne was furious!

His driver had called into the depths of his being when he saw the white flag and had beaten his opponent. Henry refused to give up the trophy but Mel was awarded the win according to the rule book.

Linne fired Mel out of his second car and the driver who had slowed when he saw the yellow was awarded the position he was running in at the time.

The Prize

The next night at Knoxville, Iowa, Sonny Ates had to give up his ride to his owner, Mel Kenyon. This was the car Mel had won his first Championship in. It was also a night when Mel lost another trophy. Mel had qualified sixth quick with his old car and on the thirty-fifth lap of the feature passed Tat and led to the checkered.

After the race, Merle Bettenhausen filed a protest that Kenyon had passed him on a yellow flag as they approached a spinning Chuck Arnold.

Merle's protest was upheld and Mel was placed third behind Tat and Bettenhausen.

The ceremonies were long over when the protest was settled and Kenyon walked over to the Honker II's pit and gave the trophy to Tat.

Mel did not win again until a month later at Hales Corner, Wisconsin.

Tat won Knoxville and Springfield. He should have stayed home from Valley Park, Missouri and Haubstadt, Indiana. He was fourth at Joliet, won Oxford, Indiana and started the July 4th weekend with a seventh at Valley Park. July 4th would be celebrated at little Springfield!

If the "Nuttley Boards" was the showplace of the 30's, Little Springfield was the midget track of the 60's and 70's. Joe Shaheen's speed bowl of dirt was a pit dug out of the earth. It was called a short quarter and Gary Bettenhausen had turned it in 12.26 seconds.

When it rained, the tow cars had to be winched out of the track which was banked on the straights as well as the turns.

Mel Kenyon and Bob Tattersall had thrilled the Springfield fans as they powerslid up the steep turns and caromed off the wooden fence made from railroad ties which circled the track.

Bob Wente would win the race and another driver destined to go to Australia with Tat, would join him at the local hospital on this night. Merle Bettenhausen, the second son of old friend Tony Bettenhausen, was the other driver.

It was a terrible looking crash. The two cars without the new cages locked together then separated. Tat's Honker II barrel rolled on top of the backstretch wall while Merle's car flipped end for end on top of Tat's machine.

Both drivers escaped with their lives and were back racing within two weeks. Tat hurt the shoulder he had damaged in 1957 and missed the Granite City race won by Bob Wente.

Howard Linne had a car for Tat while the Honker II was being repaired and Tat was fifth in it at Hales Corner, Wisconsin, just seven days after the nasty crash. Mel Kenyon recorded his first win since the Madison episode that night.

Tat was seventh in the Linne car at New Bremen and Jack Stroud had the Honker II ready for Avilla.

A disappointing sixteenth place was the best they could do as the car was sorted out.

On July 18th the racers returned to little Springfield. Tat's birthday was still nine days away but the fans had a cake and all the fixins for a party...and party they did as their favorite driver won the feature.

Tat was on a roll. He won the next night at Valley Park, dropped to twelfth at Granite City and saw red when Mel Kenyon won again. The next two were Tat's, at Davenport and Knoxville, Iowa.

Bob Tattersall installed a cage after the Santa Fe race. A spinning car shot into the track and almost ran over Tat in the Honker II. Tat hopes USAC will take a vote on the cage and either run everyone with them or without them. Reason for the cage is to keep the idiots out of the cockpit.[19]

Kenyon really tightened up the point battle in August

by winning four in a row. Tat didn't get into the win column again until September, but it was a good one. He won the Hut Hundred at Terre Haute where he had won the heat race twelve years before.

Dee remembers the celebration after the race. They partied at the bean dinner and Tat was so happy he told Dee she could make the trip to Italy she had always wanted to make.

The happy couple started the three hour trip to Streator with Dee driving as usual. Half-way home on Illinois 47, out in the middle of nowhere, the car ran out of gas.

"Tat. Wake up. We're out of gas!"

When he finally woke up, he asked, "Who was driving?"

"I was," replied Dee.

"The driver that runs out has to go get it," stated Tat as he rolled over in the back seat and went back to sleep.

A car with a lone man happened by quite a bit later.

"We ran out of gas," explained Dee. "My husband doesn't feel well."

While riding the twenty miles to the nearest open gas station, Dee began to ponder what was happening.

"This guy could drive me out in a field and rape me! I could be robbed and beaten!"

The longer these thoughts ran through her mind the madder she got.

"That Bob Tattersall, lying asleep back there and I could really be in trouble."

As she began to give rise to the fear growing within her, Dee's mind began to combat it. Soon she had turned it all around. "It would serve him right if I did get raped. Bet he'd be proud of himself."

The kind stranger let her out and drove off after being assured that Dee had friends close enough to come and help her get gasoline back to the car.

When they did arrive back at the disabled machine, there lay Bob Tattersall, the next USAC National Midget Champion, sound asleep without a care in the world.

The point race went down to the next to the last race. A fourth place at Phoenix clinched the 1969 Championship that was to be the longest schedule run by the USAC Midget Division.

"He'll set midget racing back ten years," remarked the midget supervisor, Bob Stroud.

He would be wrong!

Dear Dee and Bob

Although we know that Bob has already left for Australia, we
just want you to both know how thrilled we are the Championship
is your's at last.

It's a wonderful feeling to know that something you have worked so
hard for has finally been achieved, and we know, that everyone here
as well in Australia feels you have long been a champion before now.

We hope this year will be successful and you will defend your crown
in your usual competitive way.

We have hoped for this all year, and are glad now it is all over with.

Hope you both have a wonderful Holiday and 1970.

Love

Jay - Leroy

(Top) Congrats from Leroy Warriner on winning the USAC Championship.
(Lower Left) Tat had his 1959 UARA jacket altered after winning the USAC
Championship in 1969. *Dee Tattersall Collection.*
(Center Right) Tat #99 passes Roger West #87 on his way to victory at Oxford,
Indiana on June 29, 1969. *Jack Charters photo.*
(Lower Right) Bob Tattersall and Mel Kenyon. *R.N. Masser, Jr. photo.*

(Top) L to R. Jack Stroud, Tat and Bob Stroud. Winner of the Hut 100, 1969.
Rocky Rhodes photo.
(Bottom) Tat in the Honker II at Granite City 1969. *Rocky Rhodes photo.*

(Top) **Bob Tattersall at Terre Haute in 1969.** *Rocky Rhodes photo.*
(Bottom) **The drivers meeting at Terre Haute. Tat sitting in the center with sun glasses.** *Rocky Rhodes photo.*

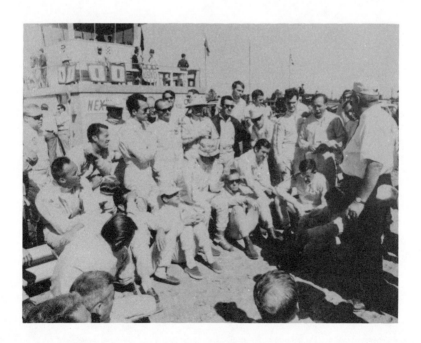

And when the chief Shepherd shall appear, you shall receive a crown of glory that fadeth not away. I Peter 5:4.

18

Defending the Crown

The USAC National Midget Champion took the Harry Conklin Offy to Australia in December of 1969. The car was out of Denver, Colorado and the suspension was changed thinking it would handle better on Australia's dirt tracks. The theory was wrong and Tat had trouble the entire tour. He did manage to win a 50 lap race in which he lapped all but the second place car. That win at Rowley Park was his last Australian victory. The best he could do in the World Derby was third after being spun out on the last lap while running second.

Stories about how sick Bob was during the spring of 1970 have proved to be in error. He partied as hard as ever and worked all season with Phil McGee to get the car right. It was not a good tour, especially for a National Champion.

During the 1970 tour Down Under Bob also suffered leg burns, which may have produced some of the stories about him not being "the same old Tat."

None of this was known when he returned to the Astrodome on March 14th.

The character of a champion is expressed in many ways. The pressure to repeat adds a new dimension to a Champion's makeup. What he is truly made of is manifested in times of trial.

The character of the 1969 USAC Champion was tested

early that spring in the shining arena of the Houston Astrodome.

Jack Stroud had the Honker II fully prepared for the rough conditions of the Astrodome's clay track. The bright yellow car carried a golden #1 designating the National Champion.

The $32,000 purse for one day's racing had everyone eager to do well.

Bob Stroud, the midget supervisor had just been released from the hospital. He had come to Houston but was far from being in shape to handle the duties of his position. As a result, the flagman, Shim Malone, would become the man in charge. Stroud would be an observer from the grandstand.

The racing surface was trucked in several days before the event and rolled as it had been the year before. No matter what was done there simply wasn't enough time to truly pack the dirt that made the banked turns.

Before the hot laps and qualifying was over the race track had already begun to break up. By feature time it was evident that there would be more holes and ruts than in the first Astro Grand Prix.

Big dollars and big names. Little guys trying to show up the Indy stars. In such a setting greed shows up. Fun times are over. Midget racing has become big business.

A J. Foyt would be hard to beat this year. He had finished second to Gary Bettenhausen in the first Astrodome race and wanted a win in his home town in the worst way.

Bruce Walkup and Bill Vukovich carried the colors for the J.C. Agajanian team. Bill Puterbaugh and Johnnie Anderson drove the Leonard Faas cars.

Indy 500 veterans made up nearly half the field. Arnie Knepper had his own car. Mike Mosley was in Continental pilot, Stan Lee's Offy. Sam Sessions drove Gene Hamilton's famous #55. Jim McElreath joined

Foyt in representing Texas with the Ed Silk car, and Bob Wente was hooked up with Sonny Knepper.

Gary Bettenhausen and Lee Kunzman were ready to win a second Astro Grand prix and Tom Bigelow, the overall winner of the first one, wanted some more of those big dollars. Three time Midget Champion, Mel Kenyon wanted his crown back. Two time Champion, Mike McGreevy joined Jimmy Caruthers and Dave Strickland as the hard charging midget stars.

The importance of the Astrodome race in midget history cannot be overlooked. For years the midgets had been almost dead. The days after World War II when midgets raced seven nights a week, to crowds numbering in the thousands, were only a memory.

The first Astro Grand Prix with 31,337 in attendance revived those glory days. This race brought attention to the midgets and purses were up because of it.

At the drivers' meeting, the drivers were told that the officials were aware of the terrible track conditions, however, they were expected to race on the track.

Twenty-six cars took Shim Malone's green flag. Within twenty laps the track surface was a mass of holes and ruts. Cars began to cut inside the tire markers to dodge the big holes in the turns.

Running on the surface itself made it impossible to keep four wheels on the ground. Those who were best prepared had softened up the shocks to absorb the impact of racing through chuck holes.

Soon drivers fighting for position found themselves running side by side over the infield tire markers.

The first warning came when cars began to hook the buried tires, ripping them out of the dirt. Within a span of five laps the race got out of hand. Steve Daily was standing on the inside of turns three and four. The cars running inside the markers had forced him back toward the infield, but in an effort to keep the cars on the track,

Steve gave ground grudgingly. After one group would come by, Steve would walk back toward the inside markers. One group running through the infield bore down on the USAC Official and cut inside to keep from running over the arm waving Daily.

The dirt infield had not been watered or treated. Dust began to fill the air. The next time around, the battling group cut the corner even deeper. It got so bad that at one point cars were on the track racing, while others were so far in the infield that Daily was trapped between them.

By the time Shim threw the red flag it was too late. The dust was so thick you could not see the backstretch.

The giant fans of the air conditioning system in the Astrodome soon cleared the dust. Unknown to the racers the giant filters in the system would all have to be replaced at the tremendous expense of $10,000.

The race was restarted with corner men holding black flags for anyone who dared to even place a wheel inside what was left of the tire markers.

In all the commotion and with eighty percent of the field cutting through the infield, one bright yellow car with a golden #1 on its tail circled the track running high and low, through ruts and holes and maintaining fifth place.

When the race was over Bob Tattersall protested the first four places who had all passed him by running through the infield. The protest was denied and Tat placed fifth.

Foyt had his victory in Houston.

Tattersall would comment, "They said I'd be a poor Champion but I raced on the track!"

The remarks made by many insiders when Bob Tattersall won the Championship rode with him during the season that was to become his last.

The midgets would not return to Houston in 1971. In

1972 A.J. Foyt would promote one more race at a reduced $10,000 purse.

The return of midget racing to the spotlight of sport faded in the dust of the Astrodome. The 77 race schedule of the 1969 season, won by Tat, would not be matched again.

In the brilliant colorful setting of the Astrodome arena, one star shone through the veil of dust, Bob Tattersall, Champion!

***

While Tat was winning his first National Title, Jimmy Caruthers was running his first season as a USAC midget driver.

Driving for his wealthy father, Jimmy had the best equipment money could buy. His first year had produced several crashes, a broken marriage and a placing of fifteenth in the point standings.

At the start of the 1970 season Doug Caruthers had purchased a new car for Jimmy to drive. Doug wanted a top chauffeur for Jimmy's old car and hoped an experienced team driver would settle his son down.

Jack Stroud was having health problems and the cost of running a car full time was more than he could handle, so Bob Tattersall became the tutor for the eager Caruthers.

Jimmy was fourth at Phoenix behind Merle Bettenhausen, Hank Butcher and Johnny Parsons, while Tat ran eighth.

The next night at Ascot Park, Jimmy lost a protested race to Bill Vukovich and Tat was third.

Dave Strickland, an ex-rodeo star, had signed with the Shannon Brothers car out of Dayton, Ohio. Long time supporters of midget racing, Gene and Bob wanted the Owners Championship in the worst way.

Tat's defense of his title would be shadowed by the

close point race between Caruthers and Strickland. The old had given way to the young.

Bob Tattersall won five features that summer. The first was at Hales Corner on June 5th. His second was twelve days later at Flamboro, Ontario, Canada.

The 100 lap feature and the Sesco engine which had grown up, but still liked to puke oil, had finished the burns received in Australia.

Tat missed five races during the hospital stay where he first met that pesky Priest. His return was at Springfield where eighth was the best he could do with his still tender feet.

The stats on the next eleven races were mixed. Fourteenth, seventh, eighth, then a win at New Bremen followed by more back of the pack races. The fourth at Minneapolis felt good as they prepared for Santa Fe Park on July 24th.

It's Tat's birthday!

Don and Sandy Carter had a huge cake made and Tat was excited as he set fast time for the night. When the rain came half-way through the show, the party moved to a tavern in Lockport and finally to the Carters' home.

Bob finished fourth in the race run the following week. There were only six more "back of the pack" finishes the rest of the year. Tat would win again at Springfield in September.

Several times Howard Linne had to supply a car while the year-old Caruthers machine was in the shop. At the Hut Hundred Bob placed eighth in the car and the Caruthers team prepared to head west.

Doug Caruthers had a second son. Young Danny was called "Kid" all of his life and he was chomping at the bit to race. "Anything Jimmy can do, I can do better."

Doug had decided that Danny was ready. Jimmy and Dave Strickland's point battle was going down to the wire and Doug wanted the second car ready in case

Jimmy's broke.

The car was going to California with one more mid-west race on the schedule, the dirt track at Bloomington, Indiana.

The chief scorer for the midget division was suffering from colitis and was to enter the hospital the next day. Ronnie Webber, who supplied the racers with tires, carried him into the booth. Years of experience allowed him to record the numbers without much realization of what was going on.

Top of the sheet, number 35. Next lap, top of the sheet, number 35.

Bob Tattersall in Gary Gamester's number 35 was winning his last USAC Feature!

The cars went west for two races at Phoenix and the Turkey Day Grand Prix at Ascot Park. Howard Linne supplied the car and Tat set fast time in the first race and won his heat. It would be his last USAC victory.

He was forty-six years old. Seven days before the race, he celebrated twenty years with Delores Ligori.

Jimmy Caruthers beat Dave Strickland by 12.48 points in a battle that went to the last race. Bob Tattersall was third in the standings. Caruthers close friend, Jerry McClung was fourth followed by Larry Rice who would later win the title for himself and for the Shannon Brothers.

(Top Left) **Tat at Springfield in 1970.**
(Top Right) **Tat #1, Barry Handlin #44 and Duke DuRosa #119.**
(Center Left) **Springfield fans.**
(Below) **A birthday party at Springfield. Left Joe Shaheen and Jim Blunk look on. Surrounded by kids Bob Stroud (hat), Tat, Jack Stroud and Steve Daily check out the cake.** *Rocky Rhodes photos.*

The teaching of the wise is a fountain of life, that one may avoid the snares of death. Proverbs 13:14.

19

Jewel in the Crown

Bob Tattersall's contribution to Australian midget racing cannot be underestimated. He was the guiding light and did so much toward the overall improvement of race equipment.

When he first started racing in Australia and New Zealand there were not too many late model speedcars in either country. "The equipment wasn't great but the Aussies and the Kiwis drove the heck out of them," Tat once told a reporter.

The situation soon changed as Bob set the standard for others to reach and the Australians and New Zealanders responded. More Offenhauser cars began to appear under local ownership, and Tat contributed by selling many of the cars he brought to Australia.

The Saylor Offy, the Cascio Offy, the Valvoline cars, the Kischell and Conklin Offenhausers all remained Down Under after Tat had completed his yearly seasonal engagements.

By the mid-sixties Australian midget racing was booming. The popularity of the sport had gone through the roof and the annual visit by Tat was the highlight of the season. The television networks in Australia were attracted to the sport and covered the weekly events at the Sydney Showground.

Bob Tattersall captured the imagination of Australian

race fans in 1965 when he told a massive TV audience his philosophy on racing.

"I just try to get to the front as quickly as I can and just keep out of the way of the rest of them. I always try to put on a show and I think that's one of the main reasons they've brought me back down here so many times, because I try to give the public what they want to see. I'm on a flat guarantee and I could just take it easy, but I don't. I'll try to win for the promoter and the people. The crowds here are fantastic. Every year they get bigger and bigger. I wish we could get that back home," Bob concluded.

Tat scored great wins in Perth, Adelaide, Melbourne, Brisbane, and in Auckland, New Zealand, but his best performances came at the Showground and earned him the title of "King of the Dirt."

Those who were able to race with Tat also became "name" drivers. Men such as Jeff Freeman, Johnny Stewart, Len Brock, Andy McGavin, Johnny Peers, Johnny Harvey, Lew Marshall, Barry Butterworth and the Cunneen Brothers all had great races with "the King."

The "World Speedcar Championship" at the Showground was the biggest event on the Down Under schedule. In its history the race has featured drivers from every country where speedcars are raced and a few where they are not. Bob Tattersall made this trophy his own private property.

"Winning the World Championship is good for me. My sponsors make a good deal out of it, so it does me good when they use it in their advertising and publicity. Winning this race is my prime objective," said Tat.

Tat won his races Down Under the hard way, from the rear of the field. His charges through traffic were always magnificent. He won the World Title in 1960, '62, '63, '65, '66, '67 and '69. In 1968 he was so far ahead he could have stopped for a hamburger and still won only to lose the engine. In 1961 he tangled with Victorian, Jack O'Dea, who at the time was at the wheel of the ex-Tattersall Saylor Offy.

Bob rode over the side of O'Dea's car and spun into the infield early in the race. Although he rejoined the race, there was no hope of winning and losing was something Tat did not take well, especially a big race on the famous Sydney Showground.

One such occasion was the 1965 Australian Speedcar Grand Prix. The date was March 6, 1965 and local Sydney star, Jeff Freeman, who had been tutored by Tat, had come from behind to defeat his teacher in what has been called the most sensational race ever run Down Under.

People still talk about the fact that after the race, which had 30,000 fans on their feet the entire distance, and after such a great display of driving from both men, Bob Tattersall did not speak to Jeff.

Everyone expected Tat to walk to Victory Lane and give him a big hug. It wasn't that Tat was mad at Jeff. Tat was mad at Tat. From those long ago days with Willie Wildhaber, losing upset him in the worst way.

The congratulations came later, at a party that night. When they came they were real and from the heart.

At the Brisbane Exhibition Ground, Tattersall's influence also had become very evident as the sixties rolled on. Brisbane became known as the "Offy Capitol of Australia."

Local idol, Blair Shepherd had initially purchased the Cascio Offy, then later had secured the ex-Don Mackay-Leroy Warriner Offenhauser, while another local star, Bill Goode was behind the wheel of the second car Jimmy Davies brought down.

Tattersall's clashes with the likes of Shepherd, Goode, Ron Wanless, Barry Valentinna, Gus McClure, Barry

Watt (who drove the ex-Mike McGreevy car) and Bob Morgan in the Kischell Offy were sensational on the tight Exhibition Ground bowl.

As 1969 arrived most of the cars in a feature at Brisbane were Offenhauser powered.

Today Phil McGee looks back with fond memories of the years he spent with Bob Tattersall. "The experience I gained around him was immense," Phil relates. "Many drivers simply steered their cars. Bob was different, he understood every part of a race car. Tat could tell in half a lap whether a change was going to improve the car or not. As crew chief, my job was made easier by his ability to communicate what the car was doing."

"Bob never made excuses or blamed his equipment unless there was really something wrong with it. He was also critical of drivers who made such excuses. Starting from the rear of the field, Bob could identify the short-comings of other drivers and could observe first hand how hard they were trying."

Phil also recalls those final days in 1971 he spent with Bob before he departed Australia for the final time.

"I spent a lot of time with Bob on his final visit. He continually passed on words of wisdom to me, just like a father. It was as if he had so much to tell me and so little time."

"He was really hoping for a miracle."

"We had made plans to run a car together in America and Australia."

"Later in 1971 I received a letter from Bob and I realized that his condition was worsening. I called him to say I was coming over to see him. Before I could go, he was gone."

The McGee Cams and Injection Company is no longer based in Sydney at the famous workshop frequented by Bob Tattersall. Many of the famous speedcar names are gone from Australia and New Zealand.

Today, Phil McGee and his younger brother, Chris, operate out of San Fernando, California, and have lived in America for sixteen years. At the entrance to their company office is a 16x20-inch photo of Bob Tattersall.

"He is there sitting in the car and ready to go."

"In our work we see him every day."

(Top) Jeff Freeman #75 on his way to the Australian Championship in 1965 passes Tat #54 and Barry Butterworth #88. *Larry Taylor photo. Nunn Collection.*
(Bottom) Sid Middlemass #54, John Stewart #98 and Tat #2 at the Sydney Showground in 1967. *Ian Smith photo. Nunn Collection.*

(Top) The World Speedcar Championship 1962. L to R. Leroy Warriner 2nd, Jeff Freeman 3rd and Bob Tattersall 1st. *Ian Smith photo. Nunn Collection.*
(Bottom) The World Speedcar Championship 1970. L to R. Tat 3rd, Ronald Mackay 2nd and Merle Bettenhausen 1st. *Ian Smith photo. Nunn Collection.*

(Top) **Jeff Freeman was driving this 2 cylinder car in the 1960 World Derby when he first met Tat. Bob going by on the outside in the Saylor Offy.**
Ian Smith photo. Nunn Collection.
(Bottom) **Ray Oram #7 Mackay Offy and Tat #12 in the Kischell Offy.**
Ian Smith photo. Nunn Collection.

Have I any pleasure at all that the wicked should die? saith the Lord God, and not that he should return from his ways and live? Ezekiel 18:23.

20

Home

A change in the promotion group at the Royale, a poor showing in 1970, rumors of illness, whatever the reason, after twelve successive years, Bob Tattersall was not on the list of drivers to be invited for the 1970-1971 season in Australia and New Zealand.

It was his old friend, Kym Bonython, who talked Mike Raymond and Frank Oliveri into bringing Tat to the Liverpool Speedway in Sydney in a joint effort with Rowley Park. For the thirteenth season Tat was back in the country he had come to love so much.

Tat had been bothered by his partial plate after the USAC season was over.

The abscess had to be scraped and he began to loose weight during the battle to make it well.

To top it all off, he suffered a terrible cut on his foot when a fifth-wheel broke on a trailer and came down on him. Mrs. Lenhausen, the registered nurse, who still lived next door, was called and wanted him to go to the hospital.

"You're a nurse. You fix it," Tat told her.

Tender loving care and butterfly bandages did the trick.

When he flew to Australia he still felt bad, but was determined to go.

Sedan (stock car) racing had taken over as the top drawcard in Australia. Remembering his start in racing, Bob Tattersall "King of the Midgets" in three countries, climbed into Ken Barlow's Falcon stock car on April 3, 1971 for the Grand National Sedan Marathon. Just eleven laps into the race the fan belt broke.

Bob remained at Liverpool for a ride in the Don Mackay Offy a week later. The main event was held in honour of Jeff Freeman. In a great race, Tat ran his long time rival, Kiwi, Barry Butterworth, to the flag but had to settle for second place.

On April 17, 1971 Bob Tattersall made his final race appearance in a midget race car. The race was "The New South Wales Speedcar Championship."

Tat placed fourth and was presented with a plaque making him a "Life Member' of the Sydney-based Eastern States Racing Association. Ashened faced he had to be helped from the car after the race.

Tat had been scheduled to drive Kym Bonython's car at Rowley Park on the 16th but the weather looked bad and he remained in Sydney. The race was rained out.

After the Liverpool race on the 17th he flew to Adelaide to prepare for a race on April 23rd.

He woke up one morning with a knot on his forehead which required immediate surgery. The news was bad!

On Saturday, May 1st, Tat flew back to Sydney to say goodbye. A pale gloom hung over the Showground arena. A carefully planned trackside interview was handled superbly by leading Australian speedway caller, Steve Raymond. Tat was then given a lap of honour in front of a standing ovation. Fellow race competitors moved from the pits to the track to accord this great American who became a legend of Australian Speedway. There was not a dry eye in the place.

An emotional Bob Tattersall watched the remainder of the meeting from the grandstand. The entire field did one slow lap waving while Tat sat silently in the stands, openly weeping.

When it was over, Tat made one final visit to the Empire Speedway's famous "Room 33" administration office, where many years earlier the track staff and promoters had enjoyed a celebration drink with him after the show.

When he arrived at the airport on Sunday he called Dee. "Dee, I'm coming home. I want to see Father John."

***

The May wind blew cold and harsh across Chicago's O'Hare field. Wheels down, flaps fully extended, the giant airplane slowly descended, crossing the spot where the huddled passenger in seat twenty-six had triumphed so many times. The O'Hare Speedway, no longer there, had been torn down for an expanded airport and progress.

Dee, Mickey and Mom were there to meet the plane. Tat refused to use a wheel chair and walked out to meet them. When they stopped to rest he told her the news.

"It's cancer."

"We struggled through the kidney, Tat, we'll struggle through this," assured Dee.

In the confines and privacy of their bedroom, the weakened warrior uttered, "Why me? Why me?"

Then silence.

Tat slept for two days after arriving home. On the third day he was wide awake and hungry.

"Where's Father John?" he asked.

"He'll be by after bit. He hasn't missed a day since you got home," Dee told him.

For the first time in his life, Bob Tattersall was afraid. Not of dying; he had spit in death's eye many a time and death had lived on his door step.

No, it wasn't death he feared. From his first day when

he had fought to see through the membrane that covered his face, he had feared nothing the outside world could throw at him. What he feared was the unknown beast within.

"Tat, Father John's here."

So began the days of searching. "Why me?" was never again uttered.

"Guess I've got the biggest race of my life, with or without a helmet, don't I?"

Father John brought the book "Achieving Peace of Mind" by a Jesuit Priest for Tat to read and began instruction in the faith.

Dee and Bob attended Kanley Catholic Church every week. For the next few months they became common everyday people.

Slowly the lessons learned so many years ago in the little brick school began to fall into place.

Little by little the "King of Down Under" became acquainted with another King. Not a weak, little baby, sissyfied King; but the King who knew of victories and cheering crowds. One who knew the labor of working with his hands, and one acquainted with grief. The one who had come to "deliver them who, through fear of death, were all their lifetime subject to bondage."

One who died the most terrible death and saw his friends forsake him.

"I've never been afraid of death. I'm not going to be now. I don't have to be."

Tat's friends did not forsake him. Bobby Grim was up every week. Mel Kenyon whose Christian life style had been so different from Tat's, joined Grim on one visit. Tat was cheered up by the visit. He now understood why Mel spoke openly and unashamed about Jesus, the Christ.

It had been one exciting life for Bob and Dee, and now that was all behind them. They were good days, those few months of peace and rest with Dee.

Cards and letters arrived every day. Many confirmed what he now knew. They also knew the God of all creation.

The memory of that first trip on the boat to Australia came back to him. Then he was headed for a wonderful and strange land. Soon he would be making a similar trip and he was getting ready.

The light he fought to see that first day; the light he always needed, was found in God's Word and in the comfort of the Priest. "Old things are passed away, all things have become new."

There was no reason to be sad. Sister Mary Martina's prayers had surely followed him and God had allowed him a great life.

If there was any sadness it was when he thought how he had cheated on Dee. She had taken the responsibility of the marriage and put up with him. He never understood that deep inside was a fear of being responsible; people he had been responsible for had died.

Dee wouldn't let him dwell on it. She loved him so much. Through his Delores he understood the promise. "I'll never leave you or forsake you."

The benefit being planned would take longer than first thought. Everyone wanted to help and it was evident that hundreds of people would be involved.

By the time the event took place, Tat was too weak to attend. There was a parade in his honor and four hundred and twenty-eight people turned out for the Benefit Dinner.

Sonny Ates said it best for the racers when interviewed at the dinner. Asked if there were any special incidents about Bob Tattersall's life that he could recall, Sonny answered, "Heck, every day was an incident."

Tat told Bobby Grim to have a drink for him, and he did.

Telegrams from President Richard Nixon, Governor Richard B. Ogilvie, senators, and friends from around the world were read. There was dancing after the gifts were presented.

Tat wanted his friends to have fun.

When the last note had sounded the crowd went home.

Life goes on! That's the way it is!

***

Danny Caruthers was one year old when Bob Tattersall began racing stock cars. In 1970 he had made up his mind to be a bigger racing star than his older brother, Jimmy.

In the last race of the 1970 season, Doug Caruthers let Danny drive Tat's car in the Turkey Day Grand Prix.

While Bob Tattersall lay at home fighting his biggest battle, the "Kid" was running off with the 1971 Midget Title.

In mid-September while plans were being made to honor Tat in Streator, the midget crews left the midwest for California with stops in Denver and Colorado Springs on the way.

In Colorado, Doug's temper caused the team mechanic, Jim Williams, to leave the team. A week later at Sacramento, Doug and Danny got into an argument over the settings for the car. After heated words, Danny left the Caruthers Racing Team.

Garry Bettenhausen took over Tat's old ride for the race at Phoenix on October 22nd setting fast time and winning the feature.

Big Rick corners second $2000 sedan victory!

BIG Rick Hunter rounds up Tasmanian charger Neville Harper (1) on his way to victory in the Tralee $2000 Grand National sedan classic. For Hunter it was the second big money production car victory on the trot, having piloted the Alan Butcher owned HG Holden V8 to a magnificent victory in the 100 lap Grand National at the Liverpool Raceway a week earlier. Report and photo coverage of the big Tralee meeting appears on page 8 of this issue.

Butterworth strikes form

COLOURFUL Sydney midgeteer Barry Butterworth is riding the crest of a wave following runaway victories in three Liverpool trophy races in successive weeks!

Driving one of the nation's top Offenhausers, formerly owned by Blair Shepherd, Barry's onslaught began when he annexed the Daily Mirror Newspapers sponsored 50 lap main event on a rain soaked track. Then followed up with a slashing win in the Jeff Freeman Memorial speedcar race, holding off a determined last minute challenge from American ace Bob Tattersall.

The former NZ champion chalked up the hat-trick with a great win in the 1971 NSW Speedcar Championship event, again slaying the field with a very professional display of wheel twisting.—Report and photo coverage starts on page 2 of this issue.

speedway

BOB TATTERSALL IN ADELAIDE HOSPITAL

VISITING American midget ace Bob Tattersall (pictured right at Liverpool Raceway) has delayed his return home for several weeks in order to seek medical treatment from a leading Adelaide specialist.

The 46-year-old former USAC champion lost over two stone in weight since he first arrived in Australia early last month and was confined to a hospital bed in Adelaide last week.

Although no details of his condition or the nature of his illness have been released, it is believed Bob has a serious respiratory ailment originally contracted during the bleak Illinois winter.

Two years ago Tattersall was hospitalised for surgery when doctors removed a cancerous kidney.

Last season it was back to hospital for skin grafting after receiving burns to his legs in a racing mishap.

A firm favourite with Aussie fans and here for his 13th Down Under tour, it is to be hoped that Bob makes a complete recovery.

Ray Oram to move to West Coast

RAY ORAM, one of the nation's better known midget pilots over the last decade, has decided to settle permanently on the West Coast.

While in Perth for a three week appearance at Claremont, Oram helped out at Mota Mart, where local Offenhauser pilot Geoff Stanton is the service manager. The firm offered the diminutive Sydney charger a permanent position with the company and Oram accepted the job.

After settling his business ties, etc., in Sydney, Oram hopes to be back in Perth early this month. Ray is related by marriage to the now retired midget driver Mick Hales.

A former apprentice jockey, Oram should prove a welcome addition to the Perth speedcar ranks.

It is hoped a competitive car can be found for Oram as he has proved a spectacular performer at Claremont. No doubt most fans would like to see him become the permanent chauffeur of the Speedway Company's Offenhauser No. 62, the car in which he set a new five lap record during his recent visit.—Ken Brown.

Rod Chessell off to England

PERTH solo rider Rod Chessell is off to try his luck in England.

Young Chessell purchased a Jawa last season and showed a lot of promise in his first few rides. His career was interrupted when he broke a wrist while acting as sidecar passenger for South Aussie charger Len Bowes.

This season, Chessell has developed into one of the up and coming stars at Claremont. He earned himself a 60 yard handicap and finished a creditable third in the City of Perth title.—Ken Brown.

Celluloid Sid to USA

TOP Liverpool super-modified driver Sid Hopping is scheduled to fly out of Sydney next week bound for America and a taste of Californian speedway racing.

Sid, who will be accompanied by his wife, will be restricting his racing activities to the Californian area.

The popular Sydney wheel twister has been interested in venturing Stateside for some time but business commitments have stopped him in the past. Sid is proprietor of a Mobilgas service station at Rydalmere, an outer Sydney suburb.

"I first became interested in going to America after speaking with Billy Anderson when he raced at Liverpool early last year and then with Billy's brother, Johnny, when he raced here recently. Billy will be arranging a car for me when I get over there."

However, Sid would like to purchase a modified and take in as many meetings as possible while in California. "If I see a car at the right price and provided it runs well, I would buy the car and bring it back to Australia. But at this stage this is not definite".

The 33-year-old pedaller does not intend to confine his racing activities to the winged machines only and is also hopeful of picking up a few sprint car drives.

Sid is keen to take a crack at the paved circuits but admits the switch to pavement will require some getting used to. "However, I'm going to try and get a few runs because we will eventually get paved tracks in Australia and it would be an advantage to have a little experience under my belt

get over there," he explained.

Depending on the success of the trip, Sid may return to the US at a later date for an extended visit and some earnest competition. "If I raced over there for two or three months, the experience gained in setting a car up and campaigning on so many different sized tracks would be very valuable," he said.

When not racing during the Stateside trip, Sid intends to capture some midget and sprint car meetings on film for Aussie fans to look at. In the past he has provided Sydney TV stations with speedway films; a service which earned him the nickname "Celluloid Sid".

All speedway fans will join us in wishing Sid and his wife an enjoyable and successful trip.

(Top Left) Streator Mayor Proclamation.
(Top Right) L to R. Bob Wente, Mom Tattersall, Mel Kenyon and Dee at the
Tattersall Benefit in 1971. *Dee Tattersall Collection.*
(Center Left) Dee looks on as Roy Brammel introduces Bobby Grim at the
Tattersall Benefit. *Dee Tattersall Collection.*
(Center Right) L to R. Duke Cook, Howard Linne, Rob Greentree, Lee
Kunzman at the Tattersall Benefit. *Dee Tattersall Collection.*
Streator, Illinois honors Bob Tattersall. *Dee Tattersall Collection.*

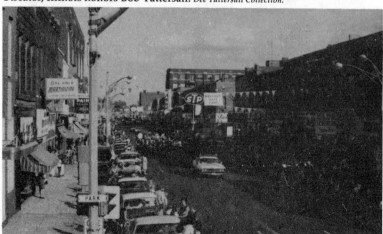

Senate Resolution No. 228

Offered by Senators Harris, Arrington, Baltz, Berning, Bidwill, Bruce, Carpentier, Carroll, Cherry, Chew, Clarke, Collins, Coulson, Course, Davidson, Donnewald, Dougherty, Egan, Fawell, Gilbert, Graham, Groen, Hall, Horsley, Hynes, Johns, Knuepfer, Knuppel, Kosinski, Kusibab, Latherow, Laughlin, Thomas G. Lyons, McBroom, McCarthy, Merritt, Mitchler, Mohr, Neistein, Newhouse, Nihill, O'Brien, Ozinga, Palmer, Partee, Rock, Romano, Rosander, Saperstein, Savickas, Smith, Soper, Sours, Swinarski, Vadalabene, Walker and Weaver.

WHEREAS, Mr. Robert Tattersall was the United States National Midget Racing Champion, and has held the Midget Racing Championship in Australia numerous times and is a national hero in the "land down under"; and

WHEREAS, Mr. Tattersall married the lovely Delores Ligori of Streator, Illinois, and now makes Streator his home; and

WHEREAS, Friday, October 15, 1971 has been designated "Bob Tattersall Day" in Streator, Illinois, in honor of this champion in their midst and the recognition he has brought to his community; and

WHEREAS, Bob Tattersall has received congratulations from the President of the United States and the State Department for being a Goodwill Ambassador to Australia and New Zealand; therefore, be it

RESOLVED, BY THE SENATE OF THE SEVENTY-SEVENTH GENERAL ASSEMBLY OF THE STATE OF ILLINOIS, that this body heartily congratulates Mr. Robert Tattersall on the happy occasion of having a day named in his honor by his home town Streator, Illinois; that we commend him for his great skill as a racing driver; that we recognize and sincerely appreciate the goodwill he has created with our nation and Australia; and that a suitable copy of this preamble and resolution be forwarded to Mr. Robert Tattersall.

Adopted by the Senate, October 14, 1971.

President of the Senate

Secretary of the Senate

For as Jonah was three days and three nights in the belly of the great fish, so shall the Son of man be three days and three nights in the heart of the earth. Matthew 12:40.

21

The Checkered Flag

For three days Tat had been too weak to speak. Father John had come by yesterday.

"Get out of here Dee! You need a break. Take off and get going. Take a couple of hours, and I don't mean down to the torch pit!"

Father John knew everything! He had been coming every day for months, reading to Tat, leaving him books and trying to give Dee some rest. He'd tell her to take off and she would go down to the torch pit and cry for an hour.

Dee decided to go to Ottawa and buy a new dress. Tat loved the way she dressed up for the races and loved to show her off. Perhaps it would cheer him up.

A planter in the shape of a casket with an unopened fifth in it sat on the table. It had been sent by "Digger"[20] when he first heard of Tat's illness.

Just after Tat had flown home from Australia he had asked Dee to become a Catholic with him. Together, they had taken the classes. Together they were baptized.

On August 17, 1971 Delores Ligori Tattersall, before God, Father John Gaughran and Robert George Tattersall, repeated the wedding vows she had worked so hard to live by since the first time she had spoken them

---

[20]Car owner, Gus Sohm.　　**199**

in November of 1950.

On August 17, 1971 Robert George Tattersall, before God, Father John Gaughran and the woman he called "his own private stock," said the marriage vows in his heart for the first time.

Doug Caruthers had replaced him. The other women no longer wanted him. The Australian promoters could no longer use him. But Dee wanted him more than ever.

The next seventy-one days were only a preview of the eternity together God promised.

Early on Tat had told Dee. "I'm not on display. Keep everyone out of my room."

Dee honored his request and only a few people were allowed in.

There were calls from friends he'd not heard from in years.

"I'm not taking visitors," he'd tell them on the phone. Even members of the family were forced to talk from the family room.

The bedroom had become his and Dee's room. Then even it became strange. Working on model semis until four in the morning Tat would say, "Take me home Dee."

"Look out the window Tat. See the wrecked cars? You are home!"

Later, "Take me home."

It wasn't the race cars now. Tat was back to the semis, back to his boyhood. Sharing the hours with his one true love, his Delores.

It was a different man who insisted on crawling out of bed to be baptized and would not celebrate the Communion except on his knees; bowing before "The King."

Twelve days ago the racers had come to the Benefit. Only Mike McGreevy was allowed into Tat's room.

"Iron" Mike, two time USAC Midget Champion, who got his nickname because he drove hard and smooth and was even tempered.

Only five feet tall, his personality and mannerly style placed him in a class with the likes of Ted Horn. He was as much at home in a tux as a driving uniform and "rowdy" wasn't in his vocabulary.

When he went into the bedroom, Mike cried like a baby. And he cussed Tat. He cussed him up one side and down the other.

He said, "You rotten............ You had the best woman in the world and all the crap you pulled in Australia. You owe her so many apologies."

He didn't know that Tat had already made his amends with Dee.

There wasn't a day that went by that Tat didn't say he was sorry. Every day Dee had told him, "You know you're forgiven."

Tat had won this one too. Now he had gotten to Mike, made him open up and speak his heart.

And there was Bucko, the former classmate whose wife had died.

"Take care of Dee. Life goes on. Don't let her go to the grave with me."

"I'll do the best I can Tat!"

***

It had been three days of silence.

Dee went into the room and spooned some water into his mouth. As she left the room to go to the kitchen, Jesus walked in.

"Tat!"

"Tat, come with me. I've got a king named David I want you to meet. You'll love him. You both have a lot in common."

Tat reached up and put his hand in the hand of the carpenter. Rising from the bed they walked from the room, headed for new adventures.

***

Doctor Mochal confirmed Tat was gone, then called the Hagi funeral home. Father John had come in and the doctor told him, "You're going to have to stay awhile. They can't get here for at least two hours."

When the doctor left, Father John told Dee to get her lessons. We still have one lesson to complete."

Together they went into Tat's room.

Dee sat in one corner and Father John in the other. Together they began the last lesson in the catechism.

Father John began, "The subject of today's lesson is THE RESURRECTION."

***

The racers poured back into Streator for the second time in two weeks. First they had come to pay tribute. Now they came to pay their respects.

The church was full. Joe Shaheen, the Springfield promoter, had come and was overwhelmed by the funeral. "I'd be so honored if I had a crowd like this at my funeral." Dee promised him she would be there.

The first song played was "My Way."

The congregation sang four songs together: "In The Garden," "Look Out Your Window," "I Believe," and Let There Be Peace On Earth."

Father John was eloquent; so much so that some in the room said if they died anytime soon, they wanted him for their funeral.

Bobby Grim, Howard Linne, Willie Wildhaber, Jack Stroud, Bob Wilkerson, Bob Higman, John Linton, and Rob Greentree acted as Honorary pallbearers.

Bob Wente, Danny Frye, Mike McGreevy, Sonny Ates, Raymond Vignochi, Frank Barsi, Howard Lopeman and Robert Knottek carried the coffin to its final resting place.

The people left the service to the sound of "You'll Never Walk Alone."

That evening while Father John was checking the church, he found an envelope tucked in the pew where the pallbearers had been seated. It read:

"Here we are, America's roughest, meanest race drivers, singing hymns and praising God, and that Bob Tattersall is probably watching us and laughing his rear off."

***

Sister Mary Martina, the nun who had taught Tat in the seventh grade and whose prayers had followed him wherever he went, stayed for the reception. In all her life she had never tasted liquor.

Dee told her it was Tat's wish that everyone have a scotch and water at the reception.

So she did!

Racing great Tattersall dies

By DAVE FALL
Auto Racing Writer

The inevitable end finally came Wednesday for Streator resident Bob Tattersall, 47, who succumbed to cancer after a four-year battle with the disease.

"Tat," who became a legend in his own time to thousands of auto racing fans throughout the United States and Australia, died at home with his wife Delores at his side.

His many accomplishments are well known. A driving veteran of 20 years, he began his career in Streator with stock cars but quickly switched to midgets, which were to become his stock and trade the rest of his life.

Bob ran for several years with Joliet's United Auto Racing Association and finished the first part of his career as the stuff. For his part in the career to attaining stardom locally with back-to-back UARA driving crowns in 1957 and 1958.

For the next dozen campaigns, Tattersall won the hearts of fans nationwide while running with the United States Auto Club.

USAC's national midget crown seemed an eternally elusive prize to him. He placed fourth in 1962, '66 and '67. In 1968, he was third. A record (at that time) 12 features were won by him in 1965 but he still finished as the runnerup.

After a decade of USAC competition, Tattersall dominated the midget division throughout 1969 to reign as the national champion, undoubtedly his greatest racing achievement. During that season he won 11 features and finished second nine times. In 1970 his last an active driver, he finished third in point standings despite being sidelined several weeks by serious foot burns.

Tattersall wake set

Funeral arrangements for racing driver Bob Tattersall were announced late Wednesday evening. Tattersall will be waked from 4 to 9 p.m. today at the Hage Funeral Home in Streator. Rosary will be read at 8 p.m.

Services for the former USAC and UARA midget champion will be held at the St. Mary's Church in Streator at 10 a.m. Friday. Burial will take place immediately following the church service at the Hillcrest Cemetary.

"Tat" was battling cancer as early as 1967. It was then that the decorated World War II paratrooper had surgery to remove a diseased kidney. Although other men would call a halt to such a demanding career following such an operation, Bob pressed on harder than ever.

Tattersall lived life the hard way and laughed at its pressures and disappointments. He was perhaps a man from another era when times were rough and driver's actions on and off the track were rougher.

The sleepless nights towing his car from one race track to another . . . the crashes and injuries one might but racing nonetheless the next night . . . the good times and parties in between. This was the life "Tat" knew and loved.

Anyone who had seen this versatile champion in action knows that a race car would have become his coffin. And if he had had his way, it probably would have been.

His 13th consecutive Australian midget campaign was suddenly interrupted last January when surgery was needed to remove a tumor from his

(continued on Page 26)

Bob Tattersall

Sister Mary Martina RSM.
1000 Paul Street
Ottawa, Illinois 61350

1024 Paul St.
Ottawa, Ill.
Oct. 14, 1971

Dear Bob,

You may not remember me but on seeing an article in the newspaper about you, I had to remind you of your seventh grade in St. Patricks, Seneca. I was your teacher. You were on the basketball team, the pride of Father Higgens, with Gene Morrow, Francis Barsi, Dale Sheedy, Fred Sheedy, Robert Milus and all the others.

It has been a long time, Bob, since we parted in June 1937 but I was happy to read of your adventurous life. It was just as I would expect it to be- full of fun, daring, spirited and successful racing.

According to Mr. Locke whom I called to get your address, you are in another race, bigger, better than ever before. This one too must be victorious, Bob, and will be. Hundreds are praying for you and I'm among them.

I hope your testimonial dinner will be a huge success . Your wife must be a valiant person, equal to her husband in courage and endurance and you both deserve the best of God s love and your friends' kindness. I won't be at your dinner but I will be waving my own checkered flag in the form of prayer. If you should win Eternity before me, please pray that I eventually get there too. I want to meet you again, Bob.

Chin up, face the future with the same toughness you've had in the past and, on meeting God, you may say as St. Paul said so long ago, " I have fought the good fight, I have finished the race, I have kept the faith. There is laid up for me a crown of justice,... the just Judge will give me and all who love His coming."

The best of everything, Bob. My prayers will be with you every day. God be with you in this race as He has been in all the others.

Devotedly

Sister Mary Martina
Sister Mary Martina

Joliet Herald News headline.
Sister Martina's letter.

BOB SWANSON   RONNEY HOUSEHOLDER   SAM HANKS   JOHNNY PARSONS SR.   JACK TURNER

SHORTY TEMPLEMAN   JIMMY DAVIES   BOB TATTERSALL   BOB WENTE SR.   MEL KENYON

Hall Of Fame Inductees Span 50 Years Of Midget Racing History

Ten outstanding midget racing drivers become the first members of the United States Auto Club Midget Racing "Hall of Fame" during inaugural ceremonies tonight.

Five drivers are from the ranks of the American Automobile Association which sanctioned various regional championships and its first national midget championship in 1948 through 1955. The United States Auto Club has been the premier sanctioning body of midget racing since 1956.

Drivers whose AAA Midget racing accomplishments have earned them their place among the initial inductees are: Johnny Parsons Sr., Sam Hanks, Ronney Householder, Bob Swanson and Jack Turner. Representing USAC in the newly-established "Hall of Fame" are: Jimmy Davies, Mel Kenyon, Bob Tattersall, Shorty Templeman and Bob Wente Sr.

Three of the four living members to be inducted into the USAC Midget Racing "Hall of Fame" will be in attendance for tonight's inaugural ceremony. Kenyon, Wente and Turner are to be inducted in person in ceremonies conducted by USAC historian Donald Davidson. Sam Hanks notified USAC he could not attend due to physician's orders.

The late Bob Tattersall will be represented by his widow, Dee. Johnny Parsons Sr., who died Sunday, is to be represented by his son Johnny Parsons Jr. The late Jimmy Davies will be represented by his son, Jimmy Davies Jr.

A permanent display containing the names of all inductees will be established at USAC headquarters in Speedway. Although tonight's initial inductees are drivers, the USAC Midget Racing "Hall of Fame" will be open to all types of participants and future inductees are expected to represent every facet of the sport.

The profiles of the inductees into the USAC Midget Racing "Hall of Fame" tonight:

Johnny Parsons Sr.

Parsons won the rain-shortened 1950 Indianapolis 500 after beginning his open wheel career in United Midget Association racing on the West Coast. Parsons won the abbreviated 1942 UMA championship on the strength of 18 feature wins. Parsons was the 1948 AAA Midwest midget champion. Parsons also was a frequent visitor at the Speedrome after retiring from racing. The popular driver and sportsman died Sunday of a heart attack in California.

Sam Hanks

Hanks captured the 1957 Indianapolis 500 in his 12th career race at the famed Speedway and announced his retirement from racing. The popular California competitor later drove the pace car at Indianapolis from 1958 through 1963. Hanks won his first midget championship in 1937 on the AMA circuit. Within the next two years, Hanks became a "barnstormer," racing on board tracks at Soldier Field in Chicago and the Los Angeles Coliseum. According to midget racing historian Jack Fox, Hanks won the first two board features at Soldier Field in 1939. Hanks won the 1949 VFW-Motor City Speedway and 1946 URA Blue Circuit championships before capturing the 1949 AAA National championship.

Ronney Householder

Householder practically raced year-round during the peak of his midget racing career,
spending the summer in the Midwest and fall and winter on the West Coast. Householder won the 1935 Detroit Coliseum race and the 1936 and 1937 Turkey Night 150-lap championship at Gilmore Stadium. Householder drove in the Indianapolis 500 in 1936 and 1937.

Bob Swanson

Swanson was the winningest driver during the colorful history of Gilmore Stadium in Los Angeles, winning the 1934 and 1938 Turkey Night midget championships and 1939 Gold Cup race there. Swanson was the 1939 Pacific Coast AAA champion. He was known as the "Blue Panther" during his years in the famed Danny Hogan Offy. Swanson did not confine his racing activities to the West Coast. He won the Madison Square Garden Bowl in Long Island. Swanson drove in three Indianapolis 500s.

Jack Turner

Turner, one of the famed northwest midget car drivers, emerged as the first two-time AAA National midget champion by winning back-to-back titles in 1954 and 1955. Turner made the entire circuit in 1954 and compiled a consistent high-finishing record to nail down the championship without the benefit of a feature win. In 1955, Turner returned to the midget racing wars and won six features. Nicknamed "Cactus Jack" because of his height and slim build, Turner later won 14 USAC National midget features under the USAC banner. He competed in six Indianapolis 500 classics and suffered a broken pelvis in a multiple-car crash on the frontstretch in which he flipped wildly in the famed Bardahl Spl.

Jimmy Davies

Davies won 46 career USAC National midget racing features, including 100-lap midget championship at the Speedrome in 1962. Davies, who added to the prestige of West Coast midget drivers, won the 1960 USAC Pacific Coast midget title. Davies became the second three-time USAC National midget champion by winning the crown in 1960, 1961 and 1962. Davies finished third in the 1955 Indianapolis 500.

Mel Kenyon

Kenyon rightfully bears the nickname "Mr. Midget" for his unprecedented accomplishments in modern-day midget car racing. The Lebanon (IN) resident is the only six-time USAC National midget champion having won the crown in 1964, 1967, 1968, 1974, 1977, and 1981. Kenyon won a milestone No. 100 career USAC National midget feature win at Kokomo Speedway in 1983. A challenger for the USAC Regional Series at the Speedrome, Kenyon won two features in 1984.

Bob Tattersall

Tattersall won the USAC National midget championship in 1969 and was a two-time runnerup for the title. Tattersall won 63 USAC national midget features during his career which attained international fame by racing in New Zealand and Australia. One of Tattersall's feature wins occured at the Speedrome in a 50-lap feature August 10, 1962.

Shorty Templeman

Templeman became the first three-time USAC National midget champion in 1958 when he added the title to his championships in 1956
and 1957. Until he finished third in the 1959 title chase, Templeman had been USAC's only national midget champion following the early years of the newly-formed sanctioning body. Templeman's local fame was increased by his popularity at the 16th Street Speedway. Templeman won 22 USAC National midget features. One of many drivers from the Northwest who continued to gain fame in the Midwest, Templeman was a five-time Washington state midget champion and three-time Oregon state midget champion.

Bob Wente Sr.

Wente won the 1963 USAC National midget championship after being a runnerup for three consecutive seasons. Wente ranks No. 2 to Kenyon in career midget wins with 78, including a 50-lap feature win at the Speedrome on Aug ust 26, 1978. Wente made his midget racing debut in 1954 with St. Louis Auto Racing Association. Wente won the USAC Midwest championship in 1960, but was nosed out of the national crown by 9.75 points by Jimmy Davies. In 1972, Wente began to devote more time to business interests than racing, although he raised four sons who are involved in racing. Nonetheless, in 1974, Wente won two features in Florida. Wente established a milestone on Aug ust 10, 1977 by qualifying for his 750th feature event, an all-time USAC record.

Postscript

On October 27, 1971 Robert George Tattersall died.

On October 29, 1971 he was laid to rest in the Hill Crest Cemetery.

The following day at race tracks around the world fans stood in a moment of silence and tribute to "The Legend."

That same day at Corona, California a determined Danny Caruthers won his heat race. He already had the 1971 USAC Championship won as he hot lapped for the feature. A stuck throttle caused the crash that slammed his head into the car's cage. Five days later he died.

Doug Caruthers accepted the award for Danny's posthumous Championship at the USAC Awards Banquet in January of 1972.

In 1975 Jimmy Caruthers, who had been tutored to the midget title by Tat, won the Championship Dirt Crown. Before the Awards Banquet was held, Jimmy died from cancer.

It was a quiet Doug Caruthers who accepted the award. He too was suffering from cancer.

Doug would win the USAC Midget Owners Championship with Rich Vogler doing the driving and would also die before the banquet honoring him.

November 13, 1971 on what would have been Tat and Dee's twenty-first anniversary, Jan Grief presented Dee with a framed copy of a poem which had been written by Bart Kotansky on the back of a beer carton. The poem has appeared in race programs around the world.

Willie Wildhaber died when his semi crashed in 1972. His last joke on the Tattersalls remains among Dee's treasures. Willie cancelled the check written for his benefit tickets.

In July 1972 the flag at the Streator VFW Post No. 1492 was flown at half-staff for the entire month in tribute to Robert Tattersall.

Frank Pavese died in 1973.

Jack Stroud joined his driver in 1978.

In 1981, Bob Tattersall was named to the UARA Hall of Fame.

In 1984, USAC named Bob among the first ten men to be inducted into the AAA/USAC Midget Hall of Fame.

For many years after his death the St. Louis Auto Racing Fan Club presented a Bob Tattersall Memorial Award during the "Nite Before the 500" midget race.

In 1991, twenty years after his death, Dee Tattersall presented the feature trophy to Steve Knepper for winning the "Bob Tattersall Memorial USAC Midget Race" at Granite City, Illinois. The promoter who escorted her across the track was Bob Wente, Jr., the young man who had been sat on by "Aunt Dee" so many years ago.

Dee was driven to Granite City by Frank "Bucko" Barsi, who has kept his promise to Tat. Though they never married, Bucko sees Dee every day and they continue to attend races.

The Ligori family still lives in the homes that surround the Ligori Scrap Yard given to them by Frank before he died in 1970.

Mom Tattersall died in 1974 while at a luncheon with Dee and Jeanette Ligori.

Midget racing continues as it always has, struggling to get back into the limelight. Like a child born with a veiled face, its young drivers and crews struggle to

emerge into the spotlight, choked back by the dust left
behind by former legends.

GOD'S SPEED

His checkered flag
Will drop no more.
Silent are the crowds
That used to roar
The asphalt crumbles
The dirt-turned to dust
The engines asleep;
Strangled with rust.
The ticket windows
A haunting scene
The concession stands —
Bare — swept clean.
The flags hang limp.
The parking lot gone.
The weeds and brush;
A sprawling lawn.
There's flowers where
The popcorn lay.

The loud speakers silent.
None to say,
"Gentlemen, start your engines".
"There's gas on the track".
"Green flags, yellow flags".
"Alright boys, bring 'em back".
Bob "Tat" Tattersall's world!
How little we know.
God, what goes through your
    mind?

Who put your finger on the button,
That determines Stop or Go?
Why this courageous gentleman?
It's unfair! Can't you see?
Why snuff his unlimited horizon?
Why couldn't you let it be?
I guess there's a reason, Lord.
You really ought to know.
But please — make sure you're
    right;

Before we let him go.
I know if Bob had to choose
He'd not have it — this way.
It'd be among the throngs of fans
Who scream and cheer and pray.
That every race a trophy
Will find its way back home
And never a nick or scratch;
A dent upon his chrome
I suppose your reasoning is good.
I can almost hear your say —
You want him all ALONE.
When you beckon that given day.
One promise God!
After you've tallied his final score!
Let him rest — content he's won —
That sprint to Heaven's Door.

Bart Kotansky

Tat the Man. 1969. *Rocky Rhodes photo.*

Bob Tattersall Race History
(outside USAC)

Sources: Joliet Herald News
Bill Hill
George Sala, Speed Sport News
Wayne Adams, Illustrated Speedway News
Paul Baines
Tony Saylor
Dee Tattersall notes

RACE HISTORY

1954 LOCATION	CLUB	#	CAR NAME	CAR OWNER	Q	H	F
5/23 87th St. Chicago	UARA						1
9/4 Joliet IL	UARA					1	
9/11 Joliet IL	UARA					1	
9/18 Joliet IL	UARA						2
9/25 Joliet IL	UARA						
9/26 LaGrange IL	UARA						

1955 LOCATION	CLUB	#	CAR NAME	CAR OWNER	Q	H	F
6/18 Joliet IL	UARA	27	Pavese Ford 60	Frank Pavese		1	
6/24 LaGrange IL	UARA	27	Pavese Ford 60	Frank Pavese		2	2
6/25 Joliet IL	UARA	27	Pavese Ford 60	Frank Pavese		1	1
7/2 Joliet IL	UARA	27	Pavese Ford 60	Frank Pavese		2	1
7/9 Joliet IL	UARA	27	Pavese Ford 60	Frank Pavese		2	1
7/31 Mazon IL	STOCK					1	4
8/7 Mazon IL	STOCK					2	cr
8/13 Joliet IL	UARA	27	Pavese Ford 60	Frank Pavese		1	1*
8/20 Joliet IL	UARA	27	Pavese Ford 60	Frank Pavese		1	
8/27 Joliet IL	UARA	27	Pavese Ford 60	Frank Pavese		1	1
9/3 Joliet IL	UARA	27	Pavese Ford 60	Frank Pavese			2
9/17 Joliet IL	UARA	27	Pavese Ford 60	Frank Pavese		2	1

*Won 4 features in row. Races rained our 4 weeks in row.

1956 LOCATION	CLUB	#	CAR NAME	CAR OWNER	Q	H	F
5/30 87th St. Chicago	UARA	27	Pavese Ford 60	Frank Pavese	1		
6/2 Joliet IL	UARA	27	Pavese Ford 60	Frank Pavese		1	3
6/9 Joliet IL	UARA	27	Pavese Ford 60	Frank Pavese	2	2	3
6/16 Joliet IL	UARA	27	Pavese Ford 60	Frank Pavese		1	
6/22 O'Hare Chicago	UARA	27	Pavese Ford 60	Frank Pavese		1	1
6/23 Joliet IL	UARA	27	Pavese Ford 60	Frank Pavese	1	1	
6/30 Joliet IL	UARA	27	Pavese Ford 60	Frank Pavese	7	1	2
7/14 Joliet IL	UARA	27	Pavese Ford 60	Frank Pavese	2	2	6
?/? O'Hare Chicago	STOCK		Mid-season				1
7/21 Joliet IL	UARA	27	Pavese Ford 60	Frank Pavese	1	1	1
7/28 Joliet IL	UARA	27	Pavese Ford 60	Frank Pavese		2	1
8/4 Joliet IL	UARA	27	Pavese Ford 60	Frank Pavese		1	1
8/9 ALTA IA	IMCA						2
8/11 Joliet IL	UARA	27	Pavese Ford 60	Frank Pavese		1	4
8/25 Joliet IL	UARA	27	Pavese Ford 60	Frank Pavese		2	1
9/1 Joliet IL	UARA	27	Pavese Ford 60	Frank Pavese		2	1
9/8 Joliet IL	UARA	27	Pavese Ford 60	Frank Pavese		1	3
9/15 Joliet IL	UARA	27	Pavese Ford 60	Frank Pavese		1	
9/16 Mazon IL	UARA	27	Pavese Ford 60	Frank Pavese		1 eng	

Q - Qualifying   H - Heat Race   F - Feature

RACE HISTORY

1957	LOCATION	CLUB	#	CAR NAME	CAR OWNER	Q	H	F
2/2	TAMPA FL	IMCA	66	MELCHER CHEVY	LEO MELCHER		2	10*
2/6	TAMPA FL	IMCA	66	MELCHER CHEVY	LEO MELCHER		2	*
2/9	TAMPA FL	IMCA	66	MELCHER CHEVY	LEO MELCHER		1	*
2/10	JACKSONVILLE FL	IMCA	66	MELCHER CHEVY	LEO MELCHER	8	3	10*
2/10	Daytona Beach FL	NASCAR	27	Pavese Ford 60	Frank Pavese	1	1	1
2/12	Daytona Beach FL	NASCAR	27	Pavese Ford 60	Frank Pavese	1	1	1
2/14	Daytona Beach FL	NASCAR	27	Pavese Ford 60	Frank Pavese	1	1	1
2/16	Daytona Beach FL	NASCAR	27	Pavese Ford 60	Frank Pavese	2	2	DNF
6/9	Santa Fe Chi	UARA	66	Saylor Offy	Tony Saylor		1	
6/21	Crown Point IN	CORA	67	Pavese Ford 60	Frank Pavese		1	1
6/22	Rockford IL	UARA	27	Pavese Ford 60	Frank Pavese		1	
6/23	Joliet IL	UARA	27	Pavese Ford 60	Frank Pavese	NTR	1	eng
6/29	Joliet IL	UARA	27	Pavese Ford 60	Frank Pavese	1	1	1
6/30	Ft. Miami OH	CSRA	69				1	14
7/4	South Bend IN	UARA	27	Pavese Ford 60	Frank Pavese	1	1	1
7/5	Crown Point IN	CORA	27	Pavese Ford 60	Frank Pavese		1	
7/6	Joliet IL	UARA	27	Pavese Ford 60	Frank Pavese	1	1	1
7/7	Alexandria IN	CORA	67	Pavese Ford 60	Frank Pavese	3	2	1
7/12	Rochester NY	NASCAR	55	Tony Saylor Offy	Tony Saylor	2	1	
7/19	Crown Point IN	CORA	67	Pavese Ford 60	Frank Pavese	1		
7/20	Joliet IL	UARA	27	Pavese Ford 60	Frank Pavese	4	3	1
7/26	Crown Point IN	CORA	67	Pavese Ford 60	Frank Pavese	3	2	1
7/27	Joliet IL	UARA	27	Pavese Ford 60	Frank Pavese	1	2	
8/	Rockford IL	UARA		Wendy's			1	cr
8/7	La CROSSE WI	IMCA					1	4
8/7	La CROSSE WI	IMCA					3	3
8/9	TIPTON IOWA	IMCA	32	FULLERTON SPL.	FULLERTON	2	3	4*
8/10	Joliet IL	UARA	27	Pavese Ford 60	Frank Pavese	6	1	1
8/11	SCHERERVILLE IN	IMCA	66	MELCHER CHEVY	LEO MELCHER	1	1	*
8/14	Cedar Rapids IA		55	Tony Saylor	Tony Saylor	5		
8/16	Crown Point IN	CORA	67	Pavese Ford 60	Frank Pavese	1	1	1
8/17	JOLIET IL	UARA	27	Pavese Ford 60	Frank Pavese	4	1	2
8/24	JOLIET IL	UARA	27	Pavese Ford 60	Frank Pavese	3	1	cr
8/31	JOLIET IL	UARA	27	Pavese Ford 60	Frank Pavese	1	2	1
9/1	Mazon IL	UARA	27	Pavese Ford 60	Frank Pavese	8	2	1
9/2	Mazon IL	UARA	27	Pavese Ford 60	Frank Pavese	NTR	2	1
9/7	Joliet IL	UARA	27	Pavese Ford 60	Frank Pavese	1	1	1
9/14	Joliet IL	UARA	27	Pavese Ford 60	Frank Pavese	2	3	1

*Sprint

Q - Qualifying   H - Heat Race   F - Feature

RACE HISTORY

1958	LOCATION	CLUB	#	CAR NAME	CAR OWNER	Q	H	F
2/8	Hollywood FL	NASCAR	55	Saylor Offy	Tony Saylor	3	2	2
2/9	W. Palm Beach FL	NASCAR	55	Saylor Offy	Tony Saylor		3	2
2/15	TAMPA FL	IMCA	66	MELCHER CHEVY	LEO MELCHER			5*
2/16	Daytona Beach FL	NASCAR	55	Saylor Offy	Tony Saylor	1	3	2
2/18	Daytona Beach FL	NASCAR	55	Saylor Offy	Tony Saylor	5	1	
2/20	Daytona Beach FL	NASCAR	55	Saylor Offy	Tony Saylor	5	1	
2/21	Daytona Beach FL	NASCAR	55	Saylor Offy	Tony Saylor	2	3	
5/13	Flint MI	CSRA	55	Saylor Offy	Tony Saylor			1
5/27	Islip NY	NASCAR	55	Saylor Offy	Tony Saylor		4	3
6/13	Abbottstown PA	NASCAR	55	Saylor Offy	Tony Saylor			1
6/14	Hagerstown MD	NASCAR	55	Saylor Offy	Tony Saylor			1
6/21	Joliet IL	UARA	57	Saylor Ford 60	Tony Saylor		3	
6/28	Joliet IL	UARA	57	Saylor Ford 60	Tony Saylor		1	1
7/5	Joliet IL	UARA	57	Saylor Ford 60	Tony Saylor		1	
7/6	Abbottstown PA	NASCAR	55	Saylor Offy	Tony Saylor		1	1
7/7	Hagerstown PA	NASCAR	55	Saylor Offy	Tony Saylor			1
7/12	Joliet IL	UARA	57	Saylor Ford 60	Tony Saylor		1	3
8/2	Joliet IL	UARA	57	Saylor Ford 60	Tony Saylor		1	1
8/7	Kankakee IL	UARA	57	Saylor Ford 60	Tony Saylor			
8/9	Joliet IL	UARA	57	Saylor Ford 60	Tony Saylor		3	1
8/10	Mazon IL	UARA	57	Saylor Ford 60	Tony Saylor			1•
8/16	Joliet IL	UARA	57	Saylor Ford 60	Tony Saylor		1	1
8/17	Santa Fe Chicago	UARA	57	Saylor Ford 60	Tony Saylor	1		1
8/23	Joliet IL	UARA	57	Saylor Ford 60	Tony Saylor		1	3
8/24	Santa Fe Chicago	UARA	57	Saylor Ford 60	Tony Saylor		1	1
8/28	Mazon IL	UARA	55	Saylor Offy	Tony Saylor			1
8/30	Joliet IL	UARA	57	Saylor Ford 60	Tony Saylor		2	6
8/31	Mazon IL	UARA	57	Saylor Ford 60	Tony Saylor			1
9/1	Mazon IL	UARA	57	Saylor Ford 60	Tony Saylor	1		1
9/6	Joliet IL	UARA	57	Saylor Ford 60	Tony Saylor		2	
9/13	Joliet IL	UARA	57	Saylor Ford 60	Tony Saylor		2	2
9/14	Charleston IL	open	55	Saylor Offy	Tony Saylor	1	1	1
9/20	O'Hare Chicago	UARA	55	Saylor Offy	Tony Saylor			3
9/21	LaGrange IL	UARA	55	Saylor Offy	Tony Saylor	1	3	1
9/27	Raceway Pk Chi	UARA	55	Saylor Offy	Tony Saylor	4	3	4
9/28	Crown Point IN	CORA	55	Saylor Offy	Tony Saylor	2	1	2
11/8	Chicago Amphi	open						1

*Sprint
•250 laps
Q - Qualifying   H - Heat Race   F - Feature

RACE HISTORY

1959 LOCATION	CLUB	#	CAR NAME	CAR OWNER	Q	H	F
2/19 Daytona Beach FL	NASCAR	57	Saylor Ford 60	Tony Saylor	1	1	2
2/20 Daytona Beach FL	NASCAR	57	Saylor Ford 60	Tony Saylor	3	1	dnf
2/21 Daytona Beach FL	NASCAR	57	Saylor Ford 60	Tony Saylor	6	1	1
5/2 Joliet IL	UARA	57	Saylor Ford 60	Tony Saylor	2	1	2
5/9 Joliet IL	UARA	57	Saylor Ford 60	Tony Saylor	4	1	1
5/16 Joliet IL	UARA	57	Saylor Ford 60	Tony Saylor	5	2	3
5/30 Joliet IL	UARA	55	Saylor Offy	Tony Saylor	2	3	1
5/31 Santa Fe Chicago	UARA	55	Saylor Offy	Tony Saylor	1	1	rain
6/5 Blue Island IL	UARA	55	Saylor Offy	Tony Saylor	3	3	1
6/6 Joliet IL	UARA	57	Saylor Ford 60	Tony Saylor	3	2	6
6/7 Sterling IL	UARA	57	Saylor Ford 60	Tony Saylor	3	1	1
6/13 Islip NY	NASCAR	55	Saylor Offy	Tony Saylor			1
6/20 Riverhead NY	NASCAR	55	Saylor Offy	Tony Saylor			1
6/26 Kankakee IL	UARA	57	Saylor Ford 60	Tony Saylor	3	1	1
6/27 Joliet IL	UARA	57	Saylor Ford 60	Tony Saylor	1	1	1
7/3 Blue Island IL	UARA	55	Saylor Offy	Tony Saylor	3	5	crsh
7/4 Mazon IL	UARA	34	Saylor Offy	Tony Saylor	1	4	2
7/5 Joliet IL	UARA	57	Saylor Ford 60	Tony Saylor	8	1	1
7/10 Blue Island IL	UARA	55	Saylor Offy	Tony Saylor	1	2	1
7/11 Joliet IL	UARA	57	Saylor Ford 60	Tony Saylor	1	1	11
7/17 Blue Island IL	UARA	55	Saylor Offy	Tony Saylor	2		1
7/18 Joliet IL	UARA	57	Saylor Ford 60	Tony Saylor			crash
7/19 Rockford IL	UARA	57	Saylor Ford 60	Tony Saylor	8	3	4
7/24 Kankakee IL	UARA	57	Saylor Ford 60	Tony Saylor		3	3
7/25 Joliet IL	UARA	57	Saylor Ford 60	Tony Saylor		1	11
7/26 Santa Fe Chicago	UARA	55	Saylor Offy	Tony Saylor	TR	2	2
7/27 Springfield IL	SLARA	55	Saylor Offy	Tony Saylor			2
7/31 Blue Island IL	UARA	55	Saylor Offy	Tony Saylor	2		6
8/1 Joliet IL	UARA	57	Saylor Ford 60	Tony Saylor	8	1	1
8/2 Sterling IL	UARA	57	Saylor Ford 60	Tony Saylor	3	1	3
8/8 Joliet IL	UARA	57	Saylor Ford 60	Tony Saylor	3	1	1
8/13 Kankakee IL	UARA	57	Saylor Ford 60	Tony Saylor	4	1	1

*Races during 58 & 59 not able to date.

?/? Lancaster NY	NASCAR	55	Saylor Offy	Tony Saylor	2	1	5
?/? Indianapolis IN	CORA	57	Saylor Ford 60	Tony Saylor	1	2	1
?/? Flint MI	ARC	55	Saylor Offy	Tony Saylor			1
?/? Richmond VA	NASCAR	55	Saylor Offy	Tony Saylor			1
?/? Ashville NC	NASCAR	55	Saylor Offy	Tony Saylor			2
?/? Atlanta GA	NASCAR	55	Saylor Offy	Tony Saylor			2
?/? Columbia SC	NASCAR	55	Saylor Offy	Tony Saylor			2
?/? Manassas WV	NASCAR	55	Saylor Offy	Tony Saylor			1

1960 LOCATION	CLUB	#	CAR NAME	CAR OWNER	Q	H	F
5/14 Joliet IL	UARA	59					3

Q - Qualifying   H - Heat Race   F - Feature

USAC Race History

of Charter Member
Bob Tattersall

This history was compiled from official USAC Records by
USAC Communication Director, Dick Jordan.

AAA RACE HISTORY

1955	LOCATION	#	CAR NAME/OWNER	Q	H	F
8/9	Terre Haute, IN	27	Pavese Ford 60/F. Pavese		1	

USAC RACE HISTORY   CHARTER MEMBER

1956	LOCATION	#	CAR NAME/OWNER	Q	H	F
4/14	Knoxville, TN	27	Pavese Ford 60/F. Pavese	7	1	13
5/13	Salem, IN	27	Pavese Ford 60/F. Pavese	12	3	15
5/22	Jeffersonville, IN	27	Pavese Ford 60/F. Pavese	18		15
5/29	Indianapolis, 16th St.	66	Saylor Offy/T. Saylor		DNS	
5/29	Indianapolis, 16th St.	66	Saylor Offy/T. Saylor	50		
5/29	Indianapolis, 16th St.	66	Saylor Offy/T. Saylor	29		

1957	LOCATION	#	CAR NAME/OWNER	Q	H	F
2/22	Ft. Pierce, FL	27	Pavese Ford 60/F. Pavese	27		^{T}
2/23	Orlando, FL	27	Pavese Ford 60/F. Pavese	23	1	^{T}
2/24	Tampa, FL	27	Pavese Ford 60/F. Pavese	14	1	12^T
3/1	Hialeah, FL	27	Pavese Ford 60/F. Pavese			^{T}
3/2	Orlando, FL	27	Pavese Ford 60/F. Pavese	11	7	3^T
3/31	READING, PA	45	LITTENBERGER OFFY/GEO.,FRANCIS	7	2	12*
4/7	WILLIAMS GROVE, PA	23	PFROMMER OFFY/J. PFROMMER	2	2	9*
4/14	ATLANTA, GA	23	PFROMMER OFFY/J. PFROMMER		crash*	
5/7	Oklahoma City, OK	14	Cunningham Offy/J. Cunningham		1	3
5/10	Wichita, KS	14	Cunningham Offy/J. Cunningham		1	1
5/12	Kansas City, KS	14	Cunningham Offy/J. Cunningham		1	3
5/29	Indianapolis, 16th St.	66	Saylor Offy/T. Saylor			
6/2	Toledo, OH	64	Al's Body Shop/A. Willey	12	1	14$_{cr}$

USAC MIDGET 38th   Legend: ^{T}USAC M/Tangerine Tournament 22nd *USAC Sprint

1959	LOCATION	#	CAR NAME/OWNER	Q	H	F
7/9	Macon, IL	96	Linne Offy/H. Linne	24	1	
7/30	Macon, IL	55	Saylor Offy/T. Saylor	8	1	7
8/17	Jeffersonville, IN	55	Saylor Offy/T. Saylor	11	1	10
8/26	Peoria, IL	55	Saylor Offy/T. Saylor	12	4	6
9/5	Schererville, IN	99	Linne Offy/H. Linne	7	4	9
9/6	DuQuoin, IL	99	Linne Offy/H. Linne			4
9/15	Macon, IL	82	H. Turner/H. Turner			7
10/4	Terre Haute, IN	3	Pawl Offy/J. Pawl			2

USAC MIDGET 41st

Q - Qualifying   H - Heat Race   F - Feature

USAC RACE HISTORY

1960	LOCATION	#	CAR NAME/OWNER	Q	H	F
4/8	Austin, TX	2	Rahn Offy/L. Rahn	8	2	1
4/9	San Antonio, TX	2	Rahn Offy/L. Rahn	8	3	2
4/10	Houston, TX	2	Rahn Offy/L. Rahn	20		16
4/17	READING, PA	89	FREY OFFY/FREY			5*
4/24	LANGHORNE, PA	6	STEARLY MOTOR FRGT./STEARLY			10*
	LANGHORNE TWIN 50	6	STEARLY MOTOR FRGT./STEARLY			9*
5/1	New Bremen, OH	88	Betty J. Offy/R. Alexander		3	12
5/29	Kokomo, IN	84	Betty J. Offy/R. Alexander	13	1	3
6/3	Flint, MI	84	Betty J. Offy/R. Alexander	5	4	16
6/8	Elyria, OH	84	Betty J. Offy/R. Alexander	9	2	7
6/9	Grand Rapids, MI	84	Betty J. Offy/R. Alexander	6	1	1
6/10	Anderson, IN	84	Betty J. Offy/R. Alexander	20	2	2
6/11	Kalamazoo, MI	84	Betty J. Offy/R. Alexander	7	2	4
6/18	South Bend, IN	84	Betty J. Offy/R. Alexander	10	5	14
6/22	Painesville, OH	84	Betty J. Offy/R. Alexander	17	2	6
6/24	Columbus, OH	84	Betty J. Offy/R. Alexander	6	2	11
6/25	Kokomo, IN	84	Betty J. Offy/R. Alexander	16	2	16
6/27	Springfield, IL	84	Betty J. Offy/R. Alexander	9	4	3
6/29	Soldiers Field, Chicago	84	Betty J. Offy/R. Alexander	15	4	8
7/2	Fairbury, IL	84	Betty J. Offy/R. Alexander	13	2	13
7/8	Anderson, IN	84	Betty J. Offy/R. Alexander	21	1	
7/9	Soldiers Field, Chicago	84	Betty J. Offy/R. Alexander	10	2	8
7/13	Atlanta, GA	84	Betty J. Offy/R. Alexander	8	1	6
7/15	Birmingham, AL	84	Betty J. Offy/R. Alexander	7	1	4
7/16	Nashville, TN	84	Betty J. Offy/R. Alexander	8	1	5
7/17	Mazon, IL	84	Betty J. Offy/R. Alexander	2	4	3
7/18	Springfield, IL	84	Betty J. Offy/R. Alexander	13	5	9
7/20	Peoria, IL	84	Betty J. Offy/R. Alexander	13	1	5
7/21	Macon, IL	84	Betty J. Offy/R. Alexander	8	1	7
7/22	East Moline, IL	84	Betty J. Offy/R. Alexander	10	1	16
7/23	St. Charles, MO	84	Betty J. Offy/R. Alexander	4	3	7
7/24	Kokomo, IN	96	Linne Offy/H. Linne	3	7	12
7/27	Soldiers Field, Chicago	96	Linne Offy/H. Linne	5	4	8
7/30	Champaign, IL	99	Linne Offy/H. Linne	3	1	3
7/31	Dayton, OH	22	Shannon Bros. Offy/Gene,Bob	19	5	13
8/3	Canfield, OH	99	Linne Offy/H. Linne	18	1	15
8/4	Mt. Vernon, OH	99	Linne Offy/H. Linne	19	4	16
8/6	South Bend, IN	34	Saylor Offy/T. Saylor	7	3	14
8/13	Kokomo, IN	78		19	4	
8/23	Hartford, MI	78		12	3	17
8/24	Fairbury, IL	78		9	1	5
8/27	Milwaukee, WI	99	Linne Offy/H. Linne	2		7
9/1	Fairfield, IL	99	Linne Offy/H. Linne		1	
9/10	St. Charles, MO	99	Linne Offy/H. Linne	6	5	1
9/17	INDY CHAMP DIRT	34	TURNER/H. TURNER			DNS^c
9/18	Salem, IN	99	Linne Offy/H. Linne	13	5	10
10/1	Fairfield, IL	99	Linne Offy/H. Linne	7	1	9
10/2	Terre Haute, IN	99	Linne Offy/H. Linne			13
10/16	New Bremen, OH	96	Linne Offy/H. Linne	7	1	5
12/17	Chicago Indoor	55	Mensing/L. Mensing	7	5	1

USAC MIDGET 5th   Legend: *USAC Sprint ^cChampionship Dirt

Q - Qualifying   H - Heat Race   F - Feature

USAC RACE HISTORY

1961	LOCATION	#	CAR NAME/OWNER	Q	H	F
3/25	Chicago Amphitheater	55	Mensing/L. Mensing	9	1	6
4/30	Kansas City, MO	14	Cunningham Offy	3	8	
5/29	Kokomo, IN	4	Leader Card Offy/R. Wilkie	1	5	14
6/3	Soldiers Field, Chicago	4	Leader Card Offy/R. Wilkie	8	4	17
6/4	New Bremen, OH	4	Leader Card Offy/R. Wilkie	5	9	14
6/12	Springfield, IL	1	Davies Offy/J. Davies			15
6/18	Danville, IL	5	Leader Card Offy/R. Wilkie	17	4	17
6/29	Grand Rapids, MI	16	Leader Card Offy/A. Wesell	15	2	13
6/30	Anderson, IN	16	Leader Card Offy/A. Wesell	11	3	
7/1	Soldiers Field, Chicago	57	Saylor Ford 60/T. Saylor	20	3	
7/3	Valley View, OH	16	Leader Card Offy/A. Wesell	18	1	9
7/7	Chattanooga, TN	16	Leader Card Offy/A. Wesell	9	1	2
7/8	Nashville, TN	16	Leader Card Offy/A. Wesell	10	3	9
7/10	Springfield, IL	16	Leader Card Offy/A. Wesell	3	3	9
7/15	Columbus, OH	16	Leader Card Offy/A. Wesell	7	1	14
7/19	Louisville, KY	16	Leader Card Offy/A. Wesell	5	6	3
7/20	Galesburg, MI	16	Leader Card Offy/A. Wesell	9	5	4
7/22	South Bend, IN	16	Leader Card Offy/A. Wesell	15		16
7/30	Kokomo, IN	5	Leader Card Offy/R. Wilkie	10	6	9
8/12	Milwaukee, WI Mile	73	Hopkins Offy/G. Hopkins	32		32
8/20	Terre Haute, IN	54	Hopkins Offy/G. Hopkins	1	8	1
8/22	Hartford, MI	15	Logan Offy/B. Logan	4	2	4
8/23	Fairbury, IL	11	Bitner Offy/Bitner	16	6	
8/27	Indianapolis, IRP	15	Logan Offy/B. Logan	20	2	11

USAC MIDGET Did not run for points

Q - Qualifying   H - Heat Race   F - Feature

USAC RACE HISTORY

1962	LOCATION	#	CAR NAME/OWNER	Q	H	F
4/20	Austin, TX	65	Snook Offy/L. Snook	8	6	5
4/21	Houston, TX	65	Snook Offy/L. Snook	13	3	10
5/4	Oklahoma City, OK	65	Snook Offy/L. Snook	4	3	11
5/6	Kansas City, KS	93	Sohm Offy/G. Sohm	8	2	17
5/13	Cincinnati, OH	10	Hamm Offy/L. Hamm	3	2	3
5/29	Indianapolis, IN	99	Linne Offy/H. Linne	3		5
6/2	Rockford, IL	5	Leader Card Offy/R. Wilkie	1	1	1
6/6	Louisville, KY	99	Linne Offy/H. Linne	2	1	3
6/8	Valley View, OH	99	Linne Offy/H. Linne	5	4	4
6/10	Freeport, IL	99	Linne Offy/H. Linne	13	2	16
6/11	Springfield, IL	99	Linne Offy/H. Linne	6	4	16
6/15	Indianapolis, IN	99	Linne Offy/H. Linne	7	2	2
6/16	South Bend, IN	99	Linne Offy/H. Linne	10	2	17
6/17	Danville, IL	99	Linne Offy/H. Linne	13	1	11
6/20	Blue Island, IL	5	Leader Card Offy/R. Wilkie	8	4	17
6/30	Kokomo, IN	54	Hopkins Offy/G. Hopkins	27		
7/1	Heidelburg, PA	48	Lawther Offy/C. Lawther	6	4	2
7/3	Valley View, OH	48	Lawther Offy/C. Lawther	9	4	5
7/6	Huntsville, AL	48	Lawther Offy/C. Lawther	4	1	15
7/16	Springfield, IL	3	Lawther Offy/C. Lawther	9	2	2
7/17	Pittsfield, IL	3	Lawther Offy/C. Lawther	14	2	7
7/19	Galesburg, IL	3	Lawther Offy/C. Lawther	15	7	9
7/20	Columbus, OH	21	Pearson Offy/E. Pearson	11	4	4
7/21	South Bend, IN	3	Lawther Offy/C. Lawther	7	4	10
7/25	Raceway Pk., Chicago	3	Lawther Offy/C. Lawther	18	2	5
7/28	Champaign, IL	3	Lawther Offy/C. Lawther	15	4	10
7/29	Kokomo, IN	3	Lawther Offy/C. Lawther	3	4	1
8/4	Valley View, OH	3	Lawther Offy/C. Lawther	14	2	12
8/8	Louisville, KY	3	Lawther Offy/C. Lawther	14	2	6
8/10	Indianapolis, IN	3	Lawther Offy/C. Lawther	8	2	1
8/11	Soldiers Field, Chicago	3	Lawther Offy/C. Lawther	8	3	12
8/15	Rockford, IL	3	Lawther Offy/C. Lawther	10	2	6
8/16	Pittsfield, IL	3	Lawther Offy/C. Lawther	3	1	2
8/17	Springfield, IL	3	Lawther Offy/C. Lawther	3	1	1
8/18	Schererville, IN	3	Lawther Offy/C. Lawther	6	4	6
8/20	Winchester, IN	4	Leader Card Offy/R. Wilkie	9	1	3
8/22	Fairbury, IL	3	Lawther Offy/C. Lawther	12	1	8
8/23	Marion, OH	3	Lawther Offy/C. Lawther	8	2	13
9/1	Schererville, IN	5	Leader Card Offy/R. Wilkie	11	1	12
9/2	Mazon, IL	5	Leader Card Offy/R. Wilkie	TR	2	
9/16	Trenton, NJ Mile	5	Leader Card Offy/R. Wilkie	7		6
10/7	Terre Haute, IN	3	Lawther Offy/C. Lawther	12	5	23
10/12	Tucson, AZ	88	Baines Offy/P. Baines	6	2	4
10/13	Phoenix, AZ	88	Baines Offy/P. Baines	3	3	15
10/20	Los Angeles, CA	88	Baines Offy/P. Baines	9	4	4
10/21	San Jose, CA	21	Turner Offy/H. Turner	18	4	8
11/22	Los Angeles, CA	99	Linne Offy/H. Linne	10		4

USAC MIDGET 4th

Q - Qualifying   H - Heat Race   F - Feature

1963	LOCATION	#	CAR NAME/OWNER	Q	H	F
4/26	Toronto, Canada	22	Shannon Bros. Offy/Gene,Bob	12		5
4/28	NEW BREMEN, OH	75	WILL CO. WRECKERS/B. LOCKARD	7		1*
5/29	Indianapolis, IN	3	Mattoon Imperial Motor/P. Baines			
6/1	Columbus, OH	3	Mattoon Imperial Motor/P. Baines	12		17
6/5	Louisville, KY		Mattoon Imperial Motor/P. Baines	7		1
6/7	Valley View, OH	3	Mattoon Imperial Motor/P. Baines	11	2	8
6/8	Soldiers Field, Chicago	3	Mattoon Imperial Motor/P. Baines	20	1	
6/11	Freeport, IL	3	Mattoon Imperial Motor/P. Baines	5		4
6/12	Rockford, IL	3	Mattoon Imperial Motor/P. Baines	6	1	5
6/15	South Bend, IN	3	Mattoon Imperial Motor/P. Baines	6		3
6/16	TERRE HAUTE, IN	75	WILL CO. WRECKERS/B. LOCKARD			*
6/16	Danville, IL	3	Mattoon Imperial Motor/P. Baines	11	1	5
6/21	Saginaw, MI	3	Mattoon Imperial Motor/P. Baines	5		8
6/22	Mt. Clemens, MI	3	Mattoon Imperial Motor/P. Baines	9	1	3
6/23	LANGHORNE, PA CHAMP	27	DAYTON STEEL WHEEL gave ride to Parnelli Jones			c
6/24	Springfield, IL	3	Mattoon Imperial Motor/P. Baines	2	3	10
6/28	Columbus, IN	3	Mattoon Imperial Motor/P. Baines	3	2	1
6/30	INDIANAPOLIS, IRP	75	WILL CO. WRECKERS/B. LOCKARD	19		15*
7/3	Valley View, OH	3	Mattoon Imperial Motor/P. Baines	16	1	5
7/6	Nashville, TN	3	Mattoon Imperial Motor/P. Baines	6	2	4
7/15	Springfield, IL	3	Mattoon Imperial Motor/P. Baines	12		14
7/19	Indy Speedrome	3	Mattoon Imperial Motor/P. Baines	10		9
7/22	Belmar, NJ	3	Mattoon Imperial Motor/P. Baines	19	1	
7/23	West Lebanon, NY	3	Mattoon Imperial Motor/P. Baines	18	3	14
7/24	Islip, NY	3	Mattoon Imperial Motor/P. Baines	1		9
7/25	Seekonk, MA	3	Mattoon Imperial Motor/P. Baines	7		3
7/27	Mt. Clemens, MI	3	Mattoon Imperial Motor/P. Baines	11	1	4
8/1	St. Louis, MO	3	Mattoon Imperial Motor/P. Baines	4	2	8
8/2	Columbus, IN	3	Mattoon Imperial Motor/P. Baines	11		8
8/3	Valley View, OH	3	Mattoon Imperial Motor/P. Baines	13	1	5
8/9	Indy Speedrome	3	Mattoon Imperial Motor/P. Baines	12		14
8/10	Chicago, IL	3	Mattoon Imperial Motor/P. Baines			
8/11	TERRE HAUTE, IN	7	HOFFMAN OFFY/HOFFMAN			DNS*
8/15	St. Louis, MO	3	Mattoon Imperial Motor/P. Baines	7	1	4
8/16	Springfield, IL	3	Mattoon Imperial Motor/P. Baines	9	3	13
8/21	Fairbury, IL	3	Mattoon Imperial Motor/P. Baines	4	1	8
8/23	Belmar, NJ	3	Mattoon Imperial Motor/P. Baines	14		12
8/24	Islip, NY	3	Mattoon Imperial Motor/P. Baines	17	1	8
8/25	Watkins Glen, NY	3	Mattoon Imperial Motor/P. Baines			22
9/2	Columbus, OH	3	Mattoon Imperial Motor/P. Baines			
9/13	Anderson, IN	3	Mattoon Imperial Motor/P. Baines	10		13
9/22	Champaign, IL	49	Hare Offy/R. Hare	23	1	
10/6	Terre Haute, IN	3	Mattoon Imperial Motor/P. Baines	6		11
10/16	Albuquerque, NM	3	Mattoon Imperial Motor/P. Baines	14	2	5
10/19	Tucson, AZ	3	Mattoon Imperial Motor/P. Baines	15	3	8
10/19	Phoenix, AZ	3	Mattoon Imperial Motor/P. Baines	24	2	
10/20	Gardena, CA	3	Mattoon Imperial Motor/P. Baines	17	2	6
11/28	Gardena, CA	23	R.J.S. CONSTRUCTION/R. Shadday	6		7

USAC MIDGET 8th   Legend: *USAC Sprint 51st cChampionship Dirt

Q - Qualifying   H - Heat Race   F - Feature

USAC RACE HISTORY

1964	LOCATION	#	CAR NAME/OWNER	Q	H	F
4/11	Gardena, CA	27	Lynch Offy/C.E. Lynch	16		11
4/12	San Bernardino, CA	27	Lynch Offy/C.E. Lynch	5		3
5/9	Jeffersonville, IN	4	Leader Card Offy/R. Wilkie	16		8
5/17	Columbus, IN	54	Hopkins Offy/G. Hopkins	7	2	14
6/3	Louisville, KY	84	Hornyak Offy/S. Hornyak	16		10
6/5	Valley View, OH	84	Hornyak Offy/S. Hornyak	10		8
6/6	Chicago, IL	84	Hornyak Offy/S. Hornyak	13	3	14
6/8	Springfield, IL	25	The Honker II/J. Stroud	12	1	5
6/9	St. Louis, MO	25	The Honker II/J. Stroud	3	1	2
6/10	Lawrenceburg, IN	54	Hopkins Offy/G. Hopkins	1	2	3
6/13	Rossburg, OH	54	Hopkins Offy/G. Hopkins	3	1	3
6/19	Toronto, Canada	21	Pearson Offy/E. Pearson	20		20
6/25	Macon, IL	25	The Honker II/J. Stroud	5	1	13
6/26	Indy Speedrome	25	The Honker II/J. Stroud	20	1	
6/26	Indy Speedrome	71	Willeford Offy/B. Gallaugher	18		16
6/27	Danville, IL	25	The Honker II/J. Stroud	2	3	1
6/29	Springfield, IL	25	The Honker II/J. Stroud	5	1	15
6/30	St. Louis, MO	25	The Honker II/J. Stroud			10
7/2	Denver, CO	25	The Honker II/J. Stroud	14		5
7/3	Colorado Springs, CO	25	The Honker II/J. Stroud	10		6
7/5	Belleville, KS	25	The Honker II/J. Stroud	2	1	4
7/9	Jackson, MI	54	Hopkins Offy/G. Hopkins	5		3
7/10	Santa Fe, Chicago	54	Hopkins Offy/G. Hopkins	2	1	1
7/11	Kokomo, IN	25	The Honker II/J. Stroud	2	1	2
7/13	Springfield, IL	25	The Honker II/J. Stroud	1		15
7/17	Indy Speedrome	14	Coil Offy/W. Coil	4	1	7
7/18	South Bend, IN	29	Saylor Offy/T. Saylor	7	3	2
7/24	Lincoln, IL	54	Hopkins Offy/G. Hopkins	8	2	1
7/27	Springfield, IL	25	The Honker II/J. Stroud	6		12
7/31	Ft. Wayne, IN	29	Saylor Offy/T. Saylor	10		7
8/1	Champaign, IL	54	Hopkins Offy/G. Hopkins	1		13
8/5	Islip, NY	25	The Honker II/J. Stroud	14		6
8/7	Old Bridge, NJ	25	The Honker II/J. Stroud	burnt piston		
8/12	Peoria, IL	25	The Honker II/J. Stroud	13	2	5
8/14	Indy Speedrome	25	The Honker II/J. Stroud	18		14
8/15	Iona, MI	25	The Honker II/J. Stroud	11		16
8/19	Chicago O'Hare	96	Linne Enterprises Ltd./H. Linne	11		3
8/26	Fairbury, IL	35	The Other Honker/J. Stroud	10	3	4
8/28	Ft. Wayne, IN	35	The Other Honker/J. Stroud			
8/29	Rossburg, OH Eldora	25	The Honker II/J. Stroud	13		17
8/30	Mazon, IL	54	Hopkins Offy/G. Hopkins	14		16
9/15	DuQuoin, IL	25	The Honker II/J. Stroud	22		16
9/7	Columbus, OH	4	Leader Card Offy/R. Wilkie	3		2
9/16	Peoria, IL	25	The Honker II/J. Stroud	10		8
9/20	Winchester, IN	21	Pearson Bros./Pearson Bros.			
9/27	TRENTON, NJ	81	J. HUNT INDY ROADSTER/J. HUNT			c
10/11	Terre Haute, IN	93	Linne Enterprises Ltd./H. Linne	4		1
10/14	Albuquerque, NM	25	The Honker II/J. Stroud	4		7
10/17	Phoenix, AZ	25	The Honker II/J. Stroud	10	2	10
11/8	San Jose, CA	1x	Goff Offy/M. Goff		2	21
11/26	Gardena, CA	80	Hoff Offy/B. Hoff	19		15

USAC MIDGET 7th   Legend: ^cChampionship Roadster

Q - Qualifying   H - Heat Race   F - Feature

1965	LOCATION	#	CAR NAME/OWNER	Q	H	F
4/17	Gardena, CA	98	Bowes Seal Fast/M. Edwards	2	1	1TR
4/24	READING, PA	26	ANKENEY OFFY/J. ANKENEY	11		9*
5/2	NEW BREMEN, OH	7	WILL' CO. WRECKERS/B. LOCKARD	11		*
5/8	Jeffersonville, IN	4	Primier Fastner/B. Nowicke	9		11
5/28	Muncie, IN	4	Primier Fastner/B. Nowicke	15		17
5/29	Indy Speedrome	4	Primier Fastner/B. Nowicke	16		14
5/30	WINCHESTER, IN	7	WILL CO. WRECKERS/B. LOCKARD	16		13*
5/30	Kokomo, IN	4	Primier Fastner/B. Nowicke	3		14
6/4	Chicago O'Hare	4	Primier Fastner/B. Nowicke	8		14
6/9	Toronto, Canada	4	Primier Fastner/B. Nowicke	15		14
6/11	Valley View, OH	4	Primier Fastner/B. Nowicke	17	1	5
6/12	South Bend, IN	4	Primier Fastner/B. Nowicke	2		4
6/13	TERRE HAUTE, IN	7	WILL CO. WRECKERS/B. LOCKARD	20		*
6/14	Springfield, IL	4	Primier Fastner/B. Nowicke	4		1
6/14	Springfield Twin 50	4	Primier Fastner/B. Nowicke			3
6/17	Jackson, MI	4	Primier Fastner/B. Nowicke	1	3	1
6/18	Ft. Wayne, IN	4	Primier Fastner/B. Nowicke	6	2	1
6/24	Louisville, KY	4	Primier Fastner/B. Nowicke	6		1
6/25	Santa Fe, Chicago	4	Primier Fastner/B. Nowicke	3	2	1
6/26	Kokomo, IN	4	Primier Fastner/B. Nowicke	1	2	14
6/30	Sandusky, OH	4	Primier Fastner/B. Nowicke	4	2	2
7/4	Winchester, IN	4	Primier Fastner/B. Nowicke	3	1	8
7/5	Flat Rock, MI	4	Primier Fastner/B. Nowicke	4	3	2
7/11	Macon, IL	4	Primier Fastner/B. Nowicke	4	1	1
7/12	Springfield, IL	4	Primier Fastner/B. Nowicke	1		8
7/12	Springfield Twin 50	4	Primier Fastner/B. Nowicke			6
7/14	Chicago O'Hare	4	Primier Fastner/B. Nowicke	10		5
7/21	Peoria, IL	4	Primier Fastner/B. Nowicke	3	1	1
7/23	Santa Fe, Chicago	4	Primier Fastner/B. Nowicke	2		5
7/24	Kokomo, IN	4	Primier Fastner/B. Nowicke	2	1	5
7/30	Jeffersonville, IN	4	Primier Fastner/B. Nowicke	8	1	8
7/31	Champaign, IL	4	Primier Fastner/B. Nowicke	2	2	1
8/6	Ft. Wayne, IN	4	Primier Fastner/B. Nowicke	4	3	8
8/12	Rockford, IL	4	Primier Fastner/B. Nowicke	6		3
8/13	Ionia, MI	4	Primier Fastner/B. Nowicke	6		5
8/14	Ionia, MI	4	Primier Fastner/B. Nowicke	10	1	8
8/15	Jackson, MI	4	Primier Fastner/B. Nowicke	4	1	2
8/20	Springfield, IL	4	Primier Fastner/B. Nowicke	6		1
8/20	Springfield Twin 50	4	Primier Fastner/B. Nowicke			14
8/25	Fairbury, IL	4	Primier Fastner/B. Nowicke	6		2
8/27	Ft. Wayne, IN	4	Primier Fastner/B. Nowicke	5		1
8/28	South Bend, IN	4	Primier Fastner/B. Nowicke	6		4
8/29	Mazon, IL	4	Primier Fastner/B. Nowicke	9	1	4
9/1	Chicago O'Hare	4	Primier Fastner/B. Nowicke	3	3	14
9/3	Mazon, IL	4	Primier Fastner/B. Nowicke	13	3	6
9/6	Columbus, OH	4	Primier Fastner/B. Nowicke	6		9
9/17	Anderson, IN	4	Primier Fastner/B. Nowicke	3	3	12
9/25	Springfield, IL	4	Primier Fastner/B. Nowicke	8	2	1
9/26	Indianapolis IRP	4	Primier Fastner/B. Nowicke	12		3
10/10	Terre Haute, IN	4	Primier Fastner/B. Nowicke	6		22
10/16	Gardena, CA	4	Primier Fastner/B. Nowicke	5		6
10/17	Fresno, CA	4	Primier Fastner/B. Nowicke	4	3	14
10/22	Vallejo, CA	4	Primier Fastner/B. Nowicke	7	1	16
11/20	Phoenix, AZ	4	Primier Fastner/B. Nowicke	8	1	6
11/27	Gardena, CA	4	Primier Fastner/B. Nowicke	4		18

USAC MIDGET 2nd   Legend: *USAC Sprint 37th

Q - Qualifying   H - Heat Race   F - Feature

1966	LOCATION	#	CAR NAME/OWNER	Q	H	F
5/20	INDIANAPOLIS 500	61	McMANUS BROS./D. McMANUS	ROOKIE	T†	
5/26	Muncie, IN	2	Primier Fastner/B. Nowicke		3	14
5/28	Ft. Wayne, IN	4	Primier Fastner/B. Nowicke	9	1	1
5/29	WINCHESTER, IN	12	FORBERG SPECIAL/C. FORBERG	15	14**	
5/29	Kokomo, IN	4	Primier Fastner/B. Nowicke	7	2	2
6/3	Santa Fe, Chicago	4	Primier Fastner/B. Nowicke	1		2
6/4	South Bend, IN	4	Primier Fastner/B. Nowicke	8		14
6/8	Grand Rapids, MI	4	Primier Fastner/B. Nowicke	8	3	16
6/10	Chicago O'Hare	4	Primier Fastner/B. Nowicke	13	2	10
6/11	Springfield, IL	4	Primier Fastner/B. Nowicke	2	1	1
6/17	Maple Park, IL	4	Primier Fastner/B. Nowicke	3	1	3
6/19	Louisville, KY	4	Primier Fastner/B. Nowicke	10	2	11
6/26	NEW BREMEN, OH	26	VIVIAN BUICK/D. DOTY	8		14*
7/3	ROSSBURG, OH	26	VIVIAN BUICK/D. DOTY	8		14*
7/3	Flat Rock, MI	4	Primier Fastner/B. Nowicke	7		1
7/4	Chicago O'Hare	4	Primier Fastner/B. Nowicke	19	1	8
7/8	Grand Rapids, MI	4	Primier Fastner/B. Nowicke	7	1	5
7/9	South Bend, IN	4	Primier Fastner/B. Nowicke	11		17
7/15	Santa Fe, Chicago	4	Primier Fastner/B. Nowicke	7	1	2
7/16	Springfield, IL	4	Primier Fastner/B. Nowicke	3	1	1
7/17	Granite City, IL	4	Primier Fastner/B. Nowicke	1		15
7/20	Rockford, IL	4	Primier Fastner/B. Nowicke	7		5
7/23	Soldiers Field, Chicago	4	Primier Fastner/B. Nowicke	12	2	17
7/30	Champaign, IL	4	Primier Fastner/B. Nowicke	1	2	2
7/31	Granite City, IL	4	Primier Fastner/B. Nowicke	6	2	1
8/4	Ithica, NY	4	Primier Fastner/B. Nowicke	1	3	16
8/5	Nazareth, PA	4	Primier Fastner/B. Nowicke	9	3	3
8/6	READING, PA	3nl	MATAKA BROS./MATAKA BROS.	15		10*
8/6	Allentown, PA	4	Primier Fastner/B. Nowicke	6		3
8/11	Jackson, MI	4	Primier Fastner/B. Nowicke	8	1	2
8/19	Springfield, IL	4	Primier Fastner/B. Nowicke	9		1
8/19	Springfield Twin 50	4	Primier Fastner/B. Nowicke			14
8/20	SPRINGFIELD CHAMP	84	MIDWEST MFG./C. GEHLHAUSEN			16ᶜ
8/24	Fairbury, IL	4	Primier Fastner/B. Nowicke	10		8
8/24	Fairbury Twin 50	4	Primier Fastner/B. Nowicke			7
8/27	Kokomo, IN	4	Primier Fastner/B. Nowicke	6	1	1
8/28	Mazon, IL	4	Primier Fastner/B. Nowicke	13	2	6
9/2	Chicago O'Hare	4	Primier Fastner/B. Nowicke	14	1	6
9/3	DuQuoin, IL	4	Primier Fastner/B. Nowicke	1		13
9/3	DuQuoin Twin 50	4	Primier Fastner/B. Nowicke			16
9/5	DuQUOIN CHAMP	84	MIDWEST MFG./C. GEHLHAUSEN			13ᶜ
9/10	INDIANAPOLIS CHAMP	84	MIDWEST MFG./C. GEHLHAUSEN			18ᶜ
9/9	Anderson, IN	96	Linne Racing Ent./H. Linne	6	2	1
9/11	GRANITE CITY, IL	84	MIDWEST MFG./C. GEHLHAUSEN	8		*
9/11	Granite City, IL	63	Neier/D. Neier	8		6
9/17	Dallas, TX	22	Shannon Bros. Buick/Gene,Bob	7	2	3
9/18	San Antonio, TX	22	Shannon Bros. Buick/Gene,Bob	8	2	3
9/24	San Antonio, TX	22	Shannon Bros. Buick/Gene,Bob	7		9
10/20	Reno, NV	35	The Other Honker/J. Stroud	2		18
10/21	Alamont, CA	35	The Other Honker/J. Stroud	9	1	5
10/23	SACRAMENTO CHAMP	84	MIDWEST MFG./C. GEHLHAUSEN			12ᶜ*
11/15	Fresno, CA	35	The Other Honker/J. Stroud	2	1	14
11/12	GARDENA, CA	52	BLAIR SPEED SHOP/D. BLAIR	6		7*
11/13	Gardena, CA	35	The Other Honker/J. Stroud	5	3	4
11/14	Phoenix, AZ	35	The Other Honker/J. Stroud	4	2	5
11/24	Gardena, CA	35	The Other Honker/J. Stroud	1		17

USAC MIDGET 4th   Legend: *USAC Sprint 42nd   **Rel. by Bud Randall
†Indianapolis 500 Mile Race Rookie Test Completed   ᶜChamp Dirt   ᶜ*Rel. by Ligouri

Q - Qualifying   H - Heat Race   F - Feature

USAC RACE HISTORY

1967	LOCATION	#	CAR NAME/OWNER	Q	H	F
4/7	Tucson, AZ	35	The Honker II/J. Stroud	6	3	1
4/8	Phoenix, AZ	35	The Honker II/J. Stroud	15		17
4/15	Gardena, CA	35	The Honker II/J. Stroud	1	2	8
4/22	READING, PA	26	J. ANKENEY/J. ANKENEY	6		13*
4/23	TRENTON, NJ CHAMP	52	VARGO OFFY/J. VARGO			10ᶜ
4/28	Lubbock, TX	35	The Honker II/J. Stroud	1	1	2
4/29	Lubbock, TX	35	The Honker II/J. Stroud	3	1	4
4/30	San Antonio, TX	35	The Honker II/J. Stroud	2	2	13
5/7	SALEM, IN	92	DUNSETH CHEV/P. LEFFLER			*
7/14	Hershey, PA	35	The Honker II/J. Stroud	6		18
7/16	New Bremen, OH	28	Lithgow Offy/B. Lithgow	14	3	16
7/20	Rockford, IL	35	The Honker II/J. Stroud	8	2	4
7/21	Santa Fe, Chicago	35	The Honker II/J. Stroud	11		8
7/22	Kokomo, IN	35	The Honker II/J. Stroud	5	1	14
7/29	Champaign, IL	35	The Honker II/J. Stroud	2		2
7/30	Granite City, IL	35	The Honker II/J. Stroud	6	1	1
8/6	Terre Haute, IN	35	The Honker II/J. Stroud	11		18
8/13	TERRE HAUTE, IN	84	MIDWEST MFG./C. GEHLHAUSEN	24		*
8/18	Springfield, IL	35	The Honker II/J. Stroud	1	1	2
8/23	Fairbury, IL	35	The Honker II/J. Stroud	10		8
8/23	Fairbury Twin 50	35	The Honker II/J. Stroud			2
8/25	Santa Fe, Chicago	35	The Honker II/J. Stroud	4		2
8/27	Mazon, IL	35	The Honker II/J. Stroud	6		17
9/2	DuQuoin, IL	35	The Honker II/J. Stroud	1		15
9/2	DuQuoin Twin 50	35	The Honker II/J. Stroud			1
9/3	Florence, KY	35	The Honker II/J. Stroud	7	1	1
9/4	Columbus, OH	35	The Honker II/J. Stroud	3		2
9/10	Louisville Downs, KY	35	The Honker II/J. Stroud	5	3	8
9/24	Terre Haute, IN	35	The Honker II/J. Stroud	4		4
10/7	New Bremen, OH	35	The Honker II/J. Stroud	5		2
10/7	New Bremen Twin 50	35	The Honker II/J. Stroud			1
10/8	Knoxville, TN	35	The Honker II/J. Stroud	2	1	3
10/21	Fresno, CA	12	D. Kischell/D. Kischell	7	1	7
10/28	GARDENA, CA	19	BLAIR SPEED SHOP/D. BLAIR	17		18*
11/12	El Cajon, CA	35	The Honker II/J. Stroud	12		8
11/17	Tucson, AZ	35	The Honker II/J. Stroud	7	3	3
11/18	Phoenix, AZ	35	The Honker II/J. Stroud	5	2	2
11/23	Gardena, CA	35	The Honker II/J. Stroud	10		22
USAC MIDGET 4th			Legend: *USAC Sprint 57th ᶜChampionship Dirt			

Q - Qualifying   H - Heat Race   F - Feature

1968	LOCATION	#	CAR NAME/OWNER	Q	H	F
4/6	Phoenix, AZ	6	Griffo's Fiat/F. Griffo		1	18
4/27	Ashville, NC	35	The Honker II/J. Stroud	5	2	2
4/28	Knoxville, TN	35	The Honker II/J. Stroud	5	2	6
5/12	New Bremen, OH	35	The Honker II/J. Stroud	4	1	13
6/2	Louisville, KY	35	The Honker II/J. Stroud	2	1	1
6/5	Avilla, IN	35	The Honker II/J. Stroud	6	2	1
6/7	Hales Corner, WI	35	The Honker II/J. Stroud	14	2	4
6/12	Joliet, IL	69	Will Co. Auto Wreckers/P. Padilla	2	2	17
6/15	Valley Park, MO	87	Loniewski Offy/E. Loniewski	16	3	7
6/18	Davenport, IA	96	Linne Enterprises Ltd./H. Linne	8	1	2
6/19	Sycamore, IL	96	Linne Enterprises Ltd./H. Linne	1	2	16
6/21	Santa Fe, Chicago	69	Will Co. Auto Wreckers/P. Padilla	2	1	2
6/28	Rockford, IL	69	Will Co. Auto Wreckers/P. Padilla	2	1	3
6/29	South Bend, IN	69	Will Co. Auto Wreckers/P. Padilla	3	1	15
6/30	Kokomo, In	87	Loniewski Offy/E. Loniewski	21	1	
7/4	Springfield, IL	93	Digger's Offy/G. Sohm	2	1	14
7/6	Valley Park, MO	93	Digger's Offy/G. Sohm	4	3	
7/7	Granite City, IL	93	Digger's Offy/G. Sohm	1	1	1
7/12	Hales Corner, WI	82	Turner Offy/H. Turner	23	1	
7/21	Kokomo, IN	51	Jeffrey Chev II/H. Jeffrey	12		18
7/30	Davenport, IA	93	Digger's Offy/G. Sohm	2	2	1
7/31	Knoxville, IA	93	Digger's Offy/G. Sohm	11	2	3
8/4	Terre Haute, IN	93	Digger's Offy/G. Sohm	1		3
8/7	Joliet, IL	28	Lithgow Offy/B. Lithgow	13		7
8/10	Indianapolis, IRP	93	Digger's Offy/G. Sohm	10	3	17
8/11	Cincinnati, OH	93	Digger's Offy/G. Sohm	4	1	2
8/14	Joliet, IL	28	Lithgow Offy/B. Lithgow	5		6
8/16	Springfield, IL	93	Digger's Offy/G. Sohm	2	2	3
8/21	Fairbury, IL	28	Lithgow Offy/B. Lithgow	20		
8/22	Rockford, IL	84	Weiland Tool Offy/K.V. Weiland	7		18
8/23	Santa Fe, Chicago	84	Weiland Tool Offy/K.V. Weiland	5		1
8/24	Valley Park, MO	93	Digger's Offy/G. Sohm	9	3	3
8/25	Mazon, IL	93	Digger's Offy/G. Sohm	9	2	3
9/6	Hales Corner, WI	84	Weiland Tool Offy/K.V. Weiland	21	1	
9/13	Springfield, IL	93	Digger's Offy/G. Sohm	3	3	3
9/14	Valley Park, MO	93	Digger's Offy/G. Sohm	5		5
9/21	Indianapolis IRP	93	Digger's Offy/G. Sohm	6		2
9/22	New Bremen, OH	93	Digger's Offy/G. Sohm	4		2
9/22	New Bremen Twin 50	93	Digger's Offy/G. Sohm			23
9/28	Granite City, IL	93	Digger's Offy/G. Sohm	8	1	1
11/16	Phoenix, AZ	5	Jim Gray/J. Gray	5	1	11
11/24	El Cajon, CA	5	Jim Gray/J. Gray	17		
11/28	Gardena, CA	78	King O' Lawn/L. Faas	23		23

USAC MIDGET 3rd

Q - Qualifying   H - Heat Race   F - Feature

1969	LOCATION	#	CAR NAME/OWNER	Q	H	F
3/28	Tucson, AZ	3	The Honker II/J. Stroud	4	2	4
3/29	Phoenix, AZ	3	The Honker II/J. Stroud	2	3	2
4/12	Fresno, CA	3	The Honker II/J. Stroud	12	1	15
5/3	Hershey, PA	3	The Honker II/J. Stroud	9		2
5/4	Jennerstown, PA	3	The Honker II/J. Stroud	7	3	1
5/11	Charleston, WV	3	The Honker II/J. Stroud	3	rain	
5/20	Davenport, IA	3	The Honker II/J. Stroud	1		1
5/23	Santa Fe, Chicago	3	The Honker II/J. Stroud	1	1	16
5/29	Indianapolis, IRP	3	The Honker II/J. Stroud	9	1	19
5/29	IRP Twin 50	3	The Honker II/J. Stroud			15
5/31	Kokomo, IN	3	The Honker II/J. Stroud	13	1	5
6/5	Rockford, IL	3	The Honker II/J. Stroud	2	2	5
6/11	Avilla, IN	3	The Honker II/J. Stroud	1	1	2
6/13	Jackson, MI	3	The Honker II/J. Stroud	2	1	6
6/14	Lansing, MI	3	The Honker II/J. Stroud	3	2	14
6/17	Davenport, IA	3	The Honker II/J. Stroud	1		1
6/18	Madison, WI	3	The Honker II/J. Stroud	11	2	17
6/19	Knoxville, IA	3	The Honker II/J. Stroud	1	1	1
6/20	Springfield, IL	3	The Honker II/J. Stroud	5	3	1
6/21	Valley Park, MO	3	The Honker II/J. Stroud	4		16
6/27	Haubstadt, IN	3	The Honker II/J. Stroud	1		14
6/28	Joliet, IL	96	Linne Enterprises Ltd./H. Linne	5		4
6/29	Oxford, IN	96	Linne Enterprises Ltd./H. Linne	9	2	1
7/3	Valley Park, MO	3	The Honker II/J. Stroud	5		7
7/4	Springfield, IL	3	The Honker II/J. Stroud	3		
7/11	Hales Corner, WI	93	Linne Enterprises Ltd./H. Linne	4		5
7/13	New Bremen, OH	93	Linne Enterprises Ltd./H. Linne	10		7
7/16	Avilla, IN	3	The Honker II/J. Stroud	5		16
7/18	Springfield, IL	3	The Honker II/J. Stroud	3	2	1
7/19	Valley Park, MO	3	The Honker II/J. Stroud	7		1
7/20	Granite City, IL	3	The Honker II/J. Stroud	2		12
7/22	Davenport, IA	3	The Honker II/J. Stroud	3	2	1
7/23	Knoxville, IA	3	The Honker II/J. Stroud	3	1	1
7/24	Minneapolis, MN	3	The Honker II/J. Stroud	2	3	7
7/25	Santa Fe, Chicago	3	The Honker II/J. Stroud	7	1	3
7/27	Madison, WI	3	The Honker II/J. Stroud	9		18
8/2	Indianapolis, IRP	3	The Honker II/J. Stroud	16	3	8
8/6	Kaukauna, WI	3	The Honker II/J. Stroud	6		6
8/8	Hales Corner, WI	3	The Honker II/J. Stroud	1	2	3
8/10	Cincinnati, OH	3	The Honker II/J. Stroud	2		2
8/13	Terre Haute, IN	3	The Honker II/J. Stroud	4		11
8/16	Jackson, MI	93	Linne Enterprises Ltd./H. Linne	3	1	2
8/18	Springfield, IL	69	Lockard Chev II/B. Lockard	20	1	13
8/19	Davenport, IA	28	Lithgow Offy/B. Lithgow	8	3	3
8/20	Fairbury, IL	3	The Honker II/J. Stroud	3		4
8/22	Santa Fe, Chicago	3	The Honker II/J. Stroud	10	2	4
8/23	Joliet, IL	3	The Honker II/J. Stroud	5		15
8/24	Rossburg, OH	3	The Honker II/J. Stroud	14	2	18
8/27	Madison, WI	93	Linne Enterprises Ltd./H. Linne	6	1	2
8/30	DuQuoin, IL	6	Gene White Tire/B. Nowicke	4		21
8/30	DuQuoin Twin 50	6	Gene White Tire/B. Nowicke			21

USAC RACE HISTORY

1969	LOCATION	#	CAR NAME/OWNER	Q	H	F
9/1	Columbus, OH	3	The Honker II/J. Stroud	2		11
9/6	Joliet, IL	3	The Honker II/J. Stroud	21	1	
9/11	Jefferson City, MO	3	The Honker II/J. Stroud	1	1	11
9/13	Valley Park, MO	3	The Honker II/J. Stroud	6		4
9/4	Granite City, IL	3	The Honker II/J. Stroud	3		2
9/19	Hales Corner, WI	3	The Honker II/J. Stroud	7	3	5
9/20	Indianapolis, IRP	3	The Honker II/J. Stroud	12		5
9/21	Oxford, IN	3	The Honker II/J. Stroud	1		3
9/26	San Jose, CA	4	London Offy/J. London	1	1	2
9/27	Stockton, CA	99	Stryker Offy/H. Stryker	8	2	4
9/28	Terre Haute, IN	3	The Honker II/J. Stroud	4		1
10/12	New Bremen, OH	3	The Honker II/J. Stroud	5	1	18
10/22	Navasota, TX	3	The Honker II/J. Stroud	15	1	2
10/25	Wichita Falls, TX	29	Vogler Chev II/D. Vogler	29	3	5
10/26	Oklahoma City, OK	3	The Honker II/J. Stroud	10		3
11/14	Phoenix, AZ	3	The Honker II/J. Stroud	2		4
11/27	Gardena, CA	3	The Honker II/J. Stroud	18		6
USAC MIDGET CHAMPION						

Q - Qualifying   H - Heat Race   F - Feature

1970	LOCATION	#	CAR NAME/OWNER	Q	H	F
3/4	Houston Astrodome	1	The Honker II/J. Stroud	19		5
3/27	Phoenix, AZ	16	Caruthers Offy/D. Caruthers	13	1	8
3/29	Gardena, CA	16	Caruthers Offy/D. Caruthers	1	1	3
4/3	Vallejo, CA	16	Caruthers Offy/D. Caruthers	3	2	14
4/11	Cincinnati, OH	28	Lithgow Offy/B. Lithgow	26		
4/17	Navasota, TX	66	Continental Airlines/S. Lee	2	2	2
4/18	Oklahoma City, OK	66	Continental Airlines/S. Lee	5		9
4/19	Lawton, OK	66	Continental Airlines/S. Lee	6	3	6
5/17	INDIANAPOLIS, IRP	56	J. COLVIN OFFY/J. COLVIN	8		*
5/29	Indianapolis, IRP	80	K. Johnson/K. Johnson	13	2	6
5/30	Kokomo, IN	80	K. Johnson/K. Johnson	4	1	4
6/3	Joliet, IL	1	Caruthers Sesco/D. Caruthers	17	3	18
6/5	Hales Corner, WI	1	Caruthers Sesco/D. Caruthers	9	3	1
6/11	Jefferson City, MO	1	Caruthers Sesco/D. Caruthers	5		6
6/12	Springfield, IL	1	Caruthers Sesco/D. Caruthers	3		18
6/13	Valley Park, MO	1	Caruthers Sesco/D. Caruthers	8	1	6
6/17	Flamboro, Ontario	1	Caruthers Sesco/D. Caruthers	2		1
7/3	Springfield, IL	1	The Honker II/J. Stroud	11		8
7/4	Valley Park, MO	1	Caruthers Sesco/D. Caruthers	2	1	14
7/5	Granite City, IL	1	Caruthers Sesco/D. Caruthers	5		7
7/10	Hales Corner, WI	1	Caruthers Sesco/D. Caruthers	12		8
7/12	New Bremen, OH	1	Caruthers Sesco/D. Caruthers	9	2	1
7/15	Avilla, IN	1	Caruthers Sesco/D. Caruthers	6	1	15
7/16	Indianapolis, IRP	1	Caruthers Sesco/D. Caruthers	10		14
7/17	Madison, WI	1	Caruthers Sesco/D. Caruthers	6		16
7/19	Minneapolis, MN	1	Caruthers Sesco/D. Caruthers	14	2	4
8/1	Kokomo, IN	1	Caruthers Sesco/D. Caruthers	17	1	7
8/6	Santa Fe, Chicago	1	Caruthers Sesco/D. Caruthers	1	1	4
8/7	Avilla, IN	1	Caruthers Sesco/D. Caruthers	1	2	14
8/12	Terre Haute, IN	1	Caruthers Sesco/D. Caruthers	3		4
8/14	Hales Corner, WI	1	Caruthers Sesco/D. Caruthers	3	2	5
8/15	South Bend, IN	1	Caruthers Sesco/D. Caruthers	2		3
8/19	Lima, OH	1	Caruthers Sesco/D. Caruthers	4	3	18
8/21	Springfield, IL	93	Linne Offy/H. Linne	2		9
8/23	Cortland, OH	1	Caruthers Sesco/D. Caruthers	8		6
8/26	Fairbury, IL	28	Lithgow Offy/B. Lithgow	21	1	
8/28	Santa Fe, Chicago	1	Caruthers Sesco/D. Caruthers	2		17
8/30	Sun Prairie, WI	1	Caruthers Sesco/D. Caruthers	23		
9/5	DuQuoin, IL	96	Linne Sesco/H. Linne	3		22
9/5	DuQuoin Twin 50	96	Linne Sesco/H. Linne			24
9/7	Columbus, OH	93	Linne Offy/H. Linne	18		18
9/11	Hales Corner, WI	1	Caruthers Sesco/D. Caruthers	4		7
9/18	Springfield, IL	1	Caruthers Sesco/D. Caruthers	2		1
9/20	Granite City, IL	1	Caruthers Sesco/D. Caruthers	7	3	6
9/27	Terre Haute, IN	1	Caruthers Sesco/D. Caruthers	11		8
10/3	Bloomington, IN	35	Gamester Sesco/G. Gamester	3	1	1
11/20	Phoenix, AZ	96	Linne Sesco/H. Linne	1	1	8
11/22	Phoenix, AZ	96	Linne Sesco/H. Linne	8		15
11/26	Gardena, CA	96	Linne Sesco/H. Linne	2		16

USAC MIDGET 3rd   Legend: *USAC Sprint

Q - Qualifying   H - Heat Race   F - Feature

Bob Tattersall Race History
Australia
and
New Zealand

Legend: dnf = Did not place in top 3

Australia: Dennis Newlyn
                  Frank Midgley
                  Ken Brown

New Zealand: Ernie Wansbone

WESTERN SPRINGS SPEEDWAY RACE RECORD
AUCKLAND, NEW ZEALAND

Compiled by Ernie Wansbone

1963-1964

Meeting	Race	Finish/Notes	
6	Feature	1st	
7	Feature	1st	
8	Feature	2nd	
9	Feature	1st	
10	Feature	3rd	
11	Feature	3rd	
12	Feature	1st	
13	MIDGET GRAND PRIX	1st	
20	MIDGET GRAND PRIX	1st	drove Barry Handlin V8/60

1964-1965

Meeting	Race	Finish/Notes	
5	Feature	1st	
6	Feature	1st	
7	Feature	1st	
8	Feature	1st	
9	Feature	dnf	spun out
10	Feature	1st	

1965-1966

Only raced one night in local car #76. Only placed in one event.

1966-1967

Meeting	Race	Finish/Notes	
7	Feature	1st	
8		Rained out	
9	Feature	1st	
10	Feature	1st	
11	WORLD 1/4 MILE CHAMP	1st	
12	Feature	1st	

1967-1968

Meeting	Race	Finish/Notes	
7	Feature	1st	
8	Feature	3rd	
9	Feature	1st	
	WORLD 1/4 MILE CHAMP	dnf	spun out

1968-1969

Meeting	Race	Finish/Notes
9	Feature	1st
10	Feature	4th
12	WORLD 1/4 MILE CHAMP	1st

1969-1970

Meeting	Race	Finish/Notes
8	Feature	1st
9	Feature	2nd
10	Feature	1st
11	WORLD 1/4 MILE CHAMP	2nd

TRACEY'S SPEEDWAY RACE RECORD
MELBOURNE, VICTORIA, AUSTRALIA

Compiled by Frank Midgley

1960-1961

Date	Race	Finish/Notes	
2/4/61	Speedcar Derby	3rd	1st B. Rickard. 2nd L. Warriner
2/11/61	VICTORIAN SPEEDCAR CHAMP	1st	

1961-1962

Date	Race	Finish/Notes
2/24/62	Australian Speedcar Derby	1st

CLAREMONT SPEEDWAY RACE RECORD
PERTH, WEST AUSTRALIA

Compiled by Ken Brown

1959-1960

Date	Race	Finish/Notes
2/12/60	Feature	1st

1961-1962

Date	Race	Finish/Notes	
1/12/62	Feature	1st	
	International Match Race	1st	beat Laurie Stevens
	Dash Series	1st	against Ray Clarke & Ken Hopkins
	Dash Series	1st	against Ray Clarke & Ken Hopkins
	Dash Series	2nd	against Ray Clarke & Ken Hopkins
	Dash Series	2nd	against Ray Clarke & Ken Hopkins
1/19/62	Claremont Speedcar Champ	1st	2nd Ray Clarke. 3rd Mike Harris

1962-1963

Date	Race	Finish/Notes	
1/25/63	Feature	2nd	1st Jimmy Davies. 4th Hidayuki Hirano
	Match Race	2nd	1st Jimmy Davies
2/1/63	World Speedcar Champ	1st	2nd Jimmy Davies. 3rd Rob Greentree

1965-1966

Date	Race	Finish/Notes	
1/14/66	Droppved valve in warm-ups.		
1/21/66	WA Craven Filter National	2nd	1st Sherman Cleveland
1/28/66	Feature `	1st	

1967-1968

Date	Race	Finish/Notes	
1/14/68	Match Race	2nd	1st Don Meacham (mech fail)
3/1/68	Feature	3rd	
	International Match Race		(mech fail) 1st Geoff Stanton

Even today Bob Tattersall remains the winningest American Driver at the Claremont Speedway, Western Australia with five feature wins.

Americans with four wins are: Larry Rice (Speedcar), Marshall Sargent (Super modified), Rocky Hodges (Sprint cars).

No visiting Australian has beat Tattersall's record. Garry Rush (NSW), Murray M. Hoffman (SA), and Ken Wylie (Vic) have 5 wins.

ROWLEY PARK RACE RECORD - 1958-1959
ADELAIDE, SOUTH AUSTRALIA

Compiled by Frank Midgley

DATE	RACE	FINISH NOTES
12/5/58	Scratch Heat	1st 2nd M. Hoffman 3rd D. Hogarth
	Final Heat	3rd 1st H. Neale 2nd A. Sunstrom
	Feature	crash spent night in hospital
12/12/58	Feature	2nd 1st A. Sunstrom
12/19/58	Scratch Heat	3rd 1st H. Neale 2nd B. Wigzell
	Final Heat	3rd 1st A. Sunstrom 2nd H. Neale
	Feature	spin Neale and Tattersall out lap 7
12/26/58	First Heat	1st
	S.A. SPEEDCAR CHAMP	1st 2nd J. Braendler 3rd R. Sendy
1/2/59	Second Heat	1st
	SPEEDCAR CHAMP	2nd 1st H. Neale
1/9/59	Scratch Heat	1st
	Final Heat	3rd 1st S. Elsworthy 2nd M. Hoffman
	Handicap (140 yds Tat)	2nd 1st D. Hogarth (50)
		3rd R. Sands (60)
	Match Races (points)	3rd 1st M. Hoffman 2nd H. Neale
	Feature	1st 2nd H. Neale 3rd M. Hoffman

ROWLEY PARK RACE RECORD - 1959-1960
ADELAIDE, SOUTH AUSTRALIA

DATE	RACE	FINISH NOTES
11/20/59	Handicap (140 yds Tat)	3rd 1st D. Lambert (40)
		2nd R. Sendy (120)
	Scratch Heat	1st 2nd R. Huppatz 3rd D. Lambert
	Feature	1st 2nd K. Bonython
11/27/59	Feature	3rd 1st B. Rickard 2nd K. Bonython
12/4/59	Feature	2nd 1st B. Rickard
12/12/59	Handicap (140 yds Tat)	2nd 1st D. Hogarth
	Feature	2nd 1st B. Rickard
12/18/59	Handicap (140 yds Tat)	3rd 1st B. Rickard (130)
		2nd R. Wood (70)
	Scratch Heat	3rd 1st M. Hoffman 2nd D. Hogarth
	Feature	2nd 1st D. Hogarth
1/2/60	1st Heat	1st
	3rd Heat	2nd 1st B. Rickard
	5th Heat	2nd 1st J. O'Dea
	AUSTRALIAN SPEEDCAR CHAMP	1st 2nd K. Bonython 3rd R. Goonan
1/8/60	GOLDEN FLEECE WORLD CHAMP	1st 2nd B. Rickard 3rd R. Goonan
1/22/60	Handicap (140 yds Tat)	1st 2nd D. Lambert (50)
		3rd K. Bonython (120)
	Stars Match 1.	1st
	Stars Match 2.	1st
	Stars Match 3.	1st
	Feature	3rd 1st M. Hoffman 2nd B. Rickard
1/29/60		Dropped valve early in programme

ROWLEY PARK RACE RECORD - 1960-1961
ADELAIDE, SOUTH AUSTRALIA

DATE	RACE	FINISH NOTES
1/20/61	GOLDEN FLEECE DERBY	spun lap 44 only 4 finished 1st L. Warriner
1/27/61	Stars 1 Lap Dashes	2nd 1st M. Hoffman
	Stars 1 Lap Dashes	3rd 1st B. Wigzell 2nd M. Hoffman
	Stars 1 Lap Dashes	1st
	Feature	3rd 1st R Sendy 2nd M. Hoffman

ROWLEY RACE RECORD - 1961-1962
ADELAIDE, SOUTH AUSTRALIA

DATE	RACE	FINISH NOTES
1/26/62	2nd Heat	1st
	S.A. SPEEDCAR CHAMP	4th 1st R. Wood 2nd B. Rickard 3rd R. Sendy
	Match Race	1st 2nd L. Warriner 3rd J. O'Dea
2/2/62	3rd Heat	1st
	GOLDEN FLEECE DERBY	3-wh 1st R. Wood 2nd L. Warriner
2/9/62	2 Lap Dash 1.	1st
	2 Lap Dash 2.	1st
	2 Lap Dash 3.	1st
	Handicap (120 yds Tat)	1st
	Stars Scratch	1st
	Feature	1st

ROWLEY PARK RACE RECORD - 1962-1963
ADELAIDE, SOUTH AUSTRALIA

DATE	RACE	FINISH NOTES
1/18/63	1st Heat	1st
	CRAVEN "A" S.A. CHAMP	mech fail 1st J. Davies 2nd C. Parsons
2/8/63	3rd Heat	1st
	Rick Harvey Memorial	spun 2 laps from finish 1st J. Davies
	Match Race 1.	2nd 1st J. Davies
	Match Race 2.	2nd 1st J. Davies
2/15/63	1st Heat	1st
	GOLDEN FLEECE DERBY	2nd 1st J. Davies

ROWLEY PARK RACE RECORD - 1963-1964, 1964-1965

Did Not Compete at Rowley Park

ROWLEY PARK RACE RECORD - 1965-1966
ADELAIDE, SOUTH AUSTRALIA

DATE	RACE	FINISH NOTES
2/4/66	International Match 1.	3rd 1st S. Cleveland 2nd J. Braendler
	International Match 2.	1st
	International Match 3.	1st
	CRAVEN FILTER S.A. CHAMP	crash 1st lap won by M. Hoffman
2/11/66	2nd Heat	2nd 1st R. Sendy
	GOLDEN FLEECE DERBY	2nd 1st S. Cleveland 3rd K. Bonython
2/18/66	3rd Heat	1st
	Rick Harvey Memorial	1st

ROWLEY PARK RACE RECORD - 1966-1967
ADELAIDE, SOUTH AUSTRALIA

DATE	RACE	FINISH NOTES
2/18/67	Heat	3rd 1st B. Rickard 2nd G. Benny
	CRAVEN FILTER S.A. CHAMP	Dnf 1st M. Hoffman 2nd D. Hogarth
3/3/67	GOLDEN FLEECE DERBY	3rd 1st B. Wigzell 2nd D. Hogarth

ROWLEY PARK RACE RECORD - 1967-1968
ADELAIDE, SOUTH AUSTRALIA

DATE	RACE	FINISH NOTES
2/9/68	Stars Match Race Points	1st 2nd D. Meacham 3rd B. Rickard
	GOLDEN FLEECE DERBY	1st
2/16/68	1st Heat	1st
	Match Races Points	1st 2nd D. Meacham 3rd M. Hoffman
	CRAVEN FILTER S.A. CHAMP	1st 2nd B. Wigzell 3rd K. Bonython

ROWLEY PARK RACE RECORD - 1968-1969
ADELAIDE, SOUTH AUSTRALIA

Did Not Compete at Rowley Park.

ROWLEY PARK RACE RECORD - 1969-1970
ADELAIDE, SOUTH AUSTRALIA

DATE	RACE	FINISH NOTES
2/13/70	Match Races Points	1st 2nd J. Kirk 3rd M. Bettenhausen
	GOLDEN FLEECE DERBY	1st 2nd B. Wigzell 3rd R. Oram

ROWLEY PARK RACE RECORD - 1970-1971
ADELAIDE, SOUTH AUSTRALIA

DATE	RACE	FINISH NOTES
4/16/71	Race Rained Out	Tat rescheduled for the 23rd
		Surgery in Adelaide before 23rd race

BRISBANE EXHIBITION GROUND RACE RECORD
BRISBANE-QUEENSLAND, AUSTRALIA

Compiled by Dennis Newlyn

1959-1960

Date	Race	Finish/Notes	
3/19/60	Empire Speedways Trophy	1st	Saylor Offy

1960-1961

Date	Race	Finish/Notes	
3/17/61	WORLD 1/4 MILE CHAMP	2nd	1st L. Warriner. 3rd R. Revell

1961-1962

Date	Race	Finish/Notes	
3/24/62	AUST 1/4 MILE GRAND PRIX	dnf	Cascio Offy
3/31/62	WORLD 1/4 MILE CHAMP	1st	

1962-1963

Date	Race	Finish/Notes	
3/23/63	AUST 1/4 MILE GRAND PRIX	3rd	1st J. Davies. 2nd A. Knowles
3/30/63	WORLD 1/4 MILE CHAMP	dnf	Mattoon Imperial Motors #3

1963-1964

Date	Race	Finish/Notes	
3/7/64	QUEENSLAND SPEEDCAR CHAMP	2nd	1st B. Shepherd. 3rd J. Davies
3/14/64	AUST 1/4 MILE GRAND PRIX	2nd	1st J. Freeman. 3rd B. Watt
3/21/64	WORLD 1/4 MILE CHAMP	1st	Mattoon Imperial Motors #3

1964-1965

Date	Race	Finish/Notes	
3/20/65	AUST 1/4 MILE GRAND PRIX	1st	Valvoline Offy
3/27/65	WORLD 1/4 MILE CHAMP	dnf	

1965-1966

Date	Race	Finish/Notes	
3/12/66	Golden Helmet Speedcar	1st	Stroud Offy #35
3/19/66	AUST 1/4 MILE GRAND PRIX	1st	
3/26/66	WORLD 1/4 MILE CHAMP	dnf	

BRISBANE EXHIBITION GROUND RACE RECORD
BRISBANE-QUEENSLAND, AUSTRALIA

1966-1967

Date	Race	Finish/Notes	
3/11/67	AUST 1/4 MILE GRAND PRIX	dnf	Valvoline Offy #2
3/18/67	WORLD 1/4 MILE CHAMP	1st	

1967-1968

Date	Race	Finish/Notes	
3/16/68	AUST 1/4 MILE GRAND PRIX	dnf	
3/23/68	21st "World's" CHAMP	2nd	1st B. Goode. 3rd B. Butterworth
3/30/68	KLG 30 lap Speedcar Derby	1st	Kischell Offy #12

1968-1969

Date	Race	Finish/Notes	
2/8/69	Golden Helmet Feature	1st	
2/15/69	WORLD 1/4 MILE CHAMP	dnf	Mackay Offy #76

1969-1970

Date	Race	Finish/Notes	
2/28/70	AUST 1/4 MILE GRAND PRIX	2nd	R. Wanless. 3rd J. Bell
3/7/70	WORLD 1/4 MILE CHAMP	dnf	Conklin Offy #1

BRISBANE EXHIBITION GROUND RACE SUMMARY

Starts	1st	2nd	3rd	DNF
23	9	5	1	8=23

SYDNEY SHOWGROUND RACE RECORD
SYDNEY, NSW, AUSTRALIA

Compiled by Dennis Newlyn

1959-1960

Date	Race	Finish/Notes	
3/5/60	Australian Speedcar Champ	1st	Saylor Offy #55
3/12/60	World Speedcar Champ	1st	Saylor Offy #55

1960-1961

Date	Race	Finish/Notes	
1/7/61	Feature	2nd	
1/14/61	Feature	1st	
2/25/61	WORLD SPEEDCAR CHAMP	dnf	spun out.

1961-1962

Date	Race	Finish/Notes	
12/16/61	Feature	dnf	1st L. Warriner
12/30/61	Feature	1st	Cascio Offy #5
1/6/62	Feature	1st	Cascio Offy #5
3/3/62	AUSTRALIAN GRAND PRIX	1st	
3/10/62	WORLD SPEEDCAR CHAMP	1st	
3/17/62	50 lap Speedcar Derby	1st	

1962-1963

Date	Race	Finish/Notes	
12/22/62	Feature	1st	Mattoon Motors Offy
1/5/63	Feature	1st	
3/9/63	AUSTRALIAN GRAND PRIX	2nd	1st J. Davies. 3rd P. Cunneen
3/16/63	WORLD SPEEDCAR CHAMP	1st	

1963-1964

Date	Race	Finish/Notes	
2/8/64	Feature	dnf	
2/15/64	Feature	dnf	
2/22/64	AUSTRALIAN GRAND PRIX	dnf	1st K. Morton. 2nd J. Stewart
2/29/64	WORLD SPEEDCAR CHAMP	dnf	blew tire.

1964-1965

Date	Race	Finish/Notes	
2/26/65	Craven Filter Royale	2nd	1st J. Freeman. 3rd P. Cunneen
3/6/65	AUSTRALIAN GRAND PRIX	2nd	1st J. Freeman. 3rd L. Marshall
3/13/65	WORLD SPEEDCAR CHAMP	1st	

SYDNEY SHOWGROUND RACE RECORD

1965-1966

Date	Race	Finish/Notes	
1/8/66	Feature	1st	Jack Stroud Offy
2/26/66	AUSTRALIAN GRAND PRIX	1st	
3/5/66	WORLD SPEEDCAR DERBY	1st	

1966-1967

Date	Race	Finish/Notes	
2/4/67	Feature	1st	Valvoline Offy #2
2/11/67	AUSTRALIAN GRAND PRIX	2nd	1st L. Brock. 3rd J. Stewart
2/18/67	WORLD SPEEDCAR CHAMP	1st	

1967-1968

Date	Race	Finish/Notes	
1/20/68	Feature	dnf	Kischell Offy #12
1/27/68	AUSTRALIAN GRAND PRIX	dnf	1st J. Stewart. 2nd D. Meacham
1/31/68	Speedcar International	dnf	
2/3/68	WORLD SPEEDCAR CHAMP	dnf	blew engine leading. 1st C. McClenahan

1968-1969

Date	Race	Finish/Notes	
1/25/69	Craven Filter NSW final	dnf	Mackay Offy #76
2/1/69	Feature	1st	
2/22/69	AUSTRALIAN GRAND PRIX	1st	
3/1/69	WORLD SPEEDCAR CHAMP	1st	

1969-1970

Date	Race	Finish/Notes	
1/31/70	Craven Filter final	3rd	Conklin Offy #1
2/7/70	AUSTRALIAN GRAND PRIX	3rd	1st R. Oram. 2nd R. Mackay
2/14/70	Craven Filter Grand Final	dnf	1st S. Middlemass. 2nd B. Pinchbeck
2/21/70	WORLD SPEEDCAR CHAMP	3rd	1st M. Bettenhausen. 2nd R. Mackay

SYDNEY SHOWGROUND RACE SUMMARY

Starts	1st	2nd	3rd	DNF
40	20	5	3	12=40

LIVERPOOL SPEEDWAY RACE RECORD
SYDNEY, NSW, AUSTRALIA

Compiled by Dennis Newlyn

Date	Race	Finish/Notes	
4/3/71	GRAND NAT SEDAN MARATHON	dnf	Broke fan belt. Ken Barlow Falcon
4/10/71	JEFF FREEMAN MEMORIAL	2nd	1st B. Butterworth
4/17/71	NSW SPEEDCAR CHAMPIONSHIP	4th	received Life Membership ESRA Bob Tattersall's last race.

(Top) L to R. Liverpool Raceway Promoter, Frank Oliveri, Tat, Willie Kaye, and Johnny Anderson prior to the start of the 100 lap Marlboro Grand National Sedan Race   *David Cumming photo. Mac Campbell collection.*

(Left) Bob Tattersall in the Ken Barlow Falcon. *David Cumming photo. Liverpool Raceway Photographer. Mac Campbell collection.*

Bob Tattersall in the Mackay Offy at Liverpool Raceway. This is one of the last photos taken of Tat in a race car. *David Cumming photo. Mac Campbell collection.*

PHOTOGRAPHERS
INDEX